GROWING Faith
ONE DAY AT A TIME

BY
Diane Brewer Lese

Growing Faith One Day at a Time
by Diane Brewer Lese
© Copyright 2020 Diane Brewer Lese. All rights reserved.

ISBN: 979-8-218-07786-0
(Previously: 978-1-937925-29-1. Originally published: Book Jolt)

Editor: Nancy James
Cover & Interior Design: Megan Dillon

Table of Contents

Dedicated with love to my family;
Alan, Andrea, Amy, & Jacquelyn.

Daily Scripture Reading
Allows You To
Grow Your Faith
One Day at a Time

INTRODUCTION

The children's voices buzzed with excitement as they viewed the packets of seeds. Carefully, Billy examined each seed packet. "Oh!" he thought. "This is the one I want!" He quickly picked up the seeds he desired to grow. After placing several handfuls of soil into his pot, Billy gently mixed in the enrichment blend to ensure his plant would have strong roots and a bountiful harvest.

Following the teacher's instructions, the children each dug a hole in the soil to make room for the seeds. Billy then carefully walked with his pot around the room, searching for the place it would receive the most light. He lovingly added water to foster the plant's growth. Each day he studied the plant recording his insights in a notebook as he patiently waited to see it grow.

Remember that science experiment at school when you grew a plant? Although we can compare faith to planting seeds, faith is not a scientific formula that you learn in school. It comes from a relationship with God that we must nurture to grow.

What is faith? Faith is defined [1]as *"complete trust or confidence in someone or something."* We may all want to have the kind of trust in God that gives us a strong faith, but it is not always easy to trust in a God we cannot see. So how do we grow that faith? It takes three things to have faith;

1. Trust that the person you have faith in can do what you need
2. Confidence that the person you have faith in loves you enough to do what you need
3. The actions and words needed to reinforce and build that faith

[1] Dictionary.com

To nurture and grow seeds of faith, here are the steps we will address in three sections of this book:

- God is Trustworthy and Able
- God's Love
- Faith

Just like Billy made the decision on which seeds he desired to grow, by selecting this book, you have already made the decision to grow your faith. Like Billy nurtured the plant with water, you will nurture your relationship with God as you implant God's words of living water in your heart by reading, writing, and speaking His Scripture from the daily Faith Focus. Reflecting on the evidence of God's Scripture will further nurture your relationship as God sheds light on the meaning of His words. Recording your insights, questions and prayers in a Faith notebook, will allow you to reflect on them. In the future, add to them as you continue your growth beyond the conclusion of this book. By performing the Enrichment activities, you will reinforce what you have learned thereby producing a more bountiful harvest of faith.

Read the daily devotionals in order. Each section of devotionals builds upon the next. I pray that you will increase your faith, be abundantly blessed, and enjoy the journey!

STEP 1
GOD IS TRUSTWORTHY AND ABLE

Ready, set, go! Two competitors race through the obstacle course blindfolded as they listen to the directions from their partners waiting at the goal line. *Two steps! Turn right! Stop!* Their adrenalin is pumping as they hurry on to win the race intently listening to their partner's directions. Even with an adrenalin rush, one competitor has no anxiety about running into an obstacle. He knows his partner is capable, protective, and loves him like a father, but then his partner actually is his father.

On the other side of the course, there are sounds of *Ouch! Thud! Crash!* That competitor is not so lucky. He is guided by a partner who loves him, but is his directionally challenged three-year-old granddaughter. Unfortunately, she is too small to see all the obstacles ahead. Her capabilities are no match for the competitor's father.

In this race, to go through the obstacles unscathed, the runner needs to trust in the love and capabilities of the person guiding them. They must know that they have the runner's best interest at heart. That same type of trust in God and faith is necessary if we are to run the race of life avoiding or overcoming obstacles as we go.

So, trust, what is it? Trust is defined[2] as "reliance on the integrity, strength, ability, surety of a person or thing." And what is faith? Faith, as we described it earlier, is "confidence or trust in a person or thing." To have faith in God, we need to trust in God.

- Trust that God is truthful
- Trust that God is faithful
- Trust that God can help us

[2] Dictionary.com

To build our faith in God, we first need to have more than head knowledge. We need to implant in our hearts that God is trustworthy and powerful enough to solve any problem, fulfill any dream, and guide us in every area of our life.

How do we implant that "faith" in our hearts? By reading, speaking, writing, and meditating on the Scriptures.

For the next six days, our focus will be on building faith in our hearts that God can do all these things and more. *"Now to Him who is able to do exceedingly abundantly above all that we ask or think, according to the power that works in us,"* Ephesians. 3:20.

DAY ONE

"*Jesus Christ is the same yesterday, today, and forever.*"

Hebrews 13:8

CHANGES!

1967!

What were things like in 1967? There were no ATMs or online banking. You had to go into the bank during banking hours to make deposits and withdrawals. How about GPS or even MapQuest? Nope! People had to read a paper map to find a location, which was a challenge for me. Film in the camera was the only way to take a photo, as digital cameras have only been sold since 1991[3]. Telephones were large with handsets attached to a base that plugged into a wall. There were even payphones in booths on the sidewalks! There were no such things as laptops. Computers were once as large as a room, but shrunk to the size of a personal desktop computer by 1974[4]. Where did I find all of this information? I did not find it in a big, massive encyclopedia as they would have in 1967. I found it on the Internet, of course! And all of these functions that I just described are now available on one little handheld smartphone.

If we can say anything about technology, we can surely say it is ever-changing. Changes, changes, and more changes! Before we adjust to the latest technology, we find it is practically obsolete. But there is one thing that will never change, and that is God. *"Jesus Christ is the same yesterday, today, and forever,"* Hebrews 13:8. Whatever God did in the Scriptures, whatever God did yesterday, He can and will do again tomorrow because our loving God never changes. So, when you are facing the challenges of daily life, remember who God was, who God is, and who God forever will be.

GOD IS TRUTH

"He is the Rock, His work is perfect; For all His ways are justice, A God of truth and without injustice; Righteous and upright is He."

Deuteronomy 32:4

GOD IS FAITHFUL

"Your mercy, O Lord, is in the heavens, Your faithfulness reaches to the clouds." Psalm 36:6

[3] Thoughtco.com
[4] History.com

4

GOD IS POWERFUL

"Ah, Lord God! Behold, You have made the heavens and the earth by Your great power and outstretched arm. There is nothing too hard for You."   Jeremiah 32:17

GOD IS SOVEREIGN

"The Lord has established His throne in heaven, and His kingdom rules over all."   Psalm 103:19

GOD IS MERCIFUL

"And the LORD passed by before him, and proclaimed, The LORD, The LORD God, merciful and gracious, longsuffering, and abounding in goodness and truth."   Exodus 34:6

God was, God is, and God forever will be all of these things and more for us!

REFLECTION

- Did you ever face a challenge in life where you felt God had resolved the issue? Write the problem and how God resolved it.

- Reflecting on the Scriptures above, do you believe God can resolve any issue in your life? Why or why not?

- How does Hebrews 13:8 impact your belief in God's abilities to answer your prayers?

What God has done before we
can trust that He can do again
because God never changes

FAITH FOCUS

God never changes

"Jesus Christ is the same yesterday, today, and forever,"

Hebrews 13:8

Prayer

Heavenly Father, write this Scripture on my heart as I read it out loud and write it in my Faith Notebook.

Heavenly Father, help me to see evidence of this Scripture today.

Record what you see, hear, or experience today that shows evidence of this Scripture.

"*God is not a man, that He should lie, nor a son of man, that He should repent. Has He said, and will He not do? Or has He spoken, and will He not make it good?*"

Numbers 23:19

HAPPY BIRTHDAY!

You can't see it. You can't hear it. You can't feel, taste, or smell it, but you know it is coming. What is it? Your birthday present! "Mommy, Daddy, I want this! Can I have it?" you eagerly ask. "Yes, you may have it, replied your parents, "but you have to wait for your 8th birthday." Your birthday has finally arrived as you race around the house, excited to open your long-awaited gift. With great anticipation, you open your present, "Yes!" you shout as you pump your fist and jump into the air, "I knew you would give me what I asked for!"

When someone we love says they will give us a specific gift, we are confident that we will receive it. We may not yet be able to see, hear, feel, taste, or smell it, but we know it is coming. Why? Because we have faith that they have told us the truth.

Isn't that like our requests to God? We may not be able to see, hear, feel, taste, or smell the answer to our request, but we can have faith that the answer will come. Why? Because our God who loves us, is not only faithful to His promises, but He is truthful. *"God is not a man, that He should lie, nor a son of man, that He should repent. Has He said, and will He not do? Or has He spoken, and will He not make it good?"* Numbers 23:19.

God's Word is truth, and He will do what He has promised, *"For all the promises of God in Him are Yes, and in Him Amen, to the glory of God through us,"* 2 Corinthians 1:20. When His Word promises that He will provide, then we can trust that He will provide. *"And my God shall supply all your need according to His riches in glory by Christ Jesus,"* Philippians 4:19. When His Word promises that He will save us, then we can trust that He will save us. *"That if you confess with your mouth the Lord Jesus and believe in your heart that God has raised Him from the dead, you will be saved,"* Romans 10:9. All that God has said in His Word is the truth that will prosper and accomplish His plan. *"So shall My word be that goes forth from My mouth; It shall not return to Me void, But it shall accomplish what I please, And it shall prosper in the thing for which I sent it,"* Isaiah 55:11.

So, no matter whether we see, hear, feel, taste, or smell the answer, we can trust that God in His love for us will come through. Whatever His answer is, it will be in His time and in the way that will be best for us. His Word is truth. We can depend on it.

REFLECTION

- In your own words, describe what Numbers 23:19 is saying about God.
- Do you believe God is true to His Word? Why or why not?
- Write one of your prayer requests that God answered.
- Can you find a Scripture verse to support the answer you received?

A great resource for identifying
scripture is https://www.biblegateway.com

Trust that God will always
keep His promises
because God cannot lie

FAITH FOCUS

God is always truthful

"God is not a man, that He should lie,
nor a son of man, that He should repent.
Has He said, and will He not do?
Or has He spoken, and will He not make it good?"
Numbers 23:19

PRAYER

Heavenly Father, write this Scripture on my heart as I read it out loud and write it in my Faith Notebook.

Heavenly Father, help me to see evidence of this Scripture today.

Record what you see, hear, or experience today that shows evidence of this Scripture.

DAY THREE

"*Your mercy, O Lord,
is in the heavens,*

Your faithfulness

reaches to the clouds."

Psalm 35:5

IT REACHES THE CLOUDS!

The earth vibrates under your feet and then, WHOOSH! The water explodes into the sky as it is propelled 185 feet, seemingly reaching the clouds! A fine hot mist of water rains down on everyone close by. What was that? Why you just witnessed the eruption of Old Faithful! Old Faithful is a geyser found in Yellowstone Park, Wyoming. (Also, home to Yogi Bear and his faithful sidekick Boo-Boo Bear.) Old Faithful powerfully erupts at predictable intervals sending explosions of 3,700 to 8,400 gallons of water up to 185 feet into the sky[5]. It can be counted on to erupt 20 times a day, and it is so faithful that its' eruptions can be predicted within a 10-minute variable[6]. Old Faithful truly lives up to its' name.

Besides Old Faithful, and maybe a loyal dog, who else can be counted on to be faithful? *"Therefore, know that the LORD your God, He is God, the faithful God who keeps covenant and mercy for a thousand generations with those who love Him and keep His commandments,"* Deuteronomy 7:9. Our God in His great love for us is faithful. Faithful in His covenant and His mercy. But how else is God faithful? God is faithful to His promises, *"For all the promises of God in Him are Yes, and in Him Amen, to the glory of God through us,"* 2 Corinthians 1:20. God is also faithful to be with us, *"And the LORD, He is the One who goes before you. He will be with you, He will not leave you nor forsake you; do not fear nor be dismayed,"* Deuteronomy 31:8.

Whatever God has said, you can predict that He will be faithful to accomplish it. He will do this with more power than Old Faithful and more reach than a mere 185 feet because God's faithfulness reaches to the clouds.

[5] Wikipedia
[6] MyYellowstonePark.com

REFLECTION

- What do the verses above say to you about God's faithfulness?
- Describe any evidence you have seen of God's faithfulness.
- Describe an experience in your life where you have depended upon God, and He was faithful to come through.

We can trust in God
to fulfill His Word
because God is faithful

FAITH FOCUS
God is faithful

"Your mercy, O Lord, is in the heavens;
Your faithfulness reaches to the clouds,"

Psalm 35:5

PRAYER

Heavenly Father, write this Scripture on my heart as I read it out loud and write it in my Faith Notebook.

Heavenly Father, help me to see evidence of this Scripture today.

Record what you see, hear, or experience today
that shows evidence of this Scripture.

Daily Scripture Reading
Allows You To
Grow Your Faith
One Day at a Time

" *One God and Father of all, who is above all, and through all, and in you all.*"

Ephesians 4:6

NO SURPRISES!

After weeks of planning, and attention to numerous details, and it is finally time for the secret to be revealed. You escort her through the darkened door and hear everyone yell, "Surprise! Surprise!" Everyone yells as they jump up from their hiding places! The birthday girl tries to look astonished using the expression she has practiced for days. But there is no faking it, somebody spilled the beans. How often have you been to a surprise party where the recipient was really surprised?

Just like recipients of a surprise party are usually not surprised, God is **never** surprised. He is prepared for all. He knows the future, He knows our hearts, (Acts 15:8) and He even knows our needs before we ask. *"Therefore, do not be like them. For your Father knows the things you have need of before you ask Him,"* Matthew 6:8.

God is over all things. Every little cotton pickin' thing! He misses nothing. Not a single hair from our heads falls without Him knowing it, (Luke 12:7). Men may try to manipulate or control the situation, but God is still sovereign, *"One God and Father of all, who is above all, and through all, and in you all,"* Ephesians 4:6.

In Daniel 3, let's look at Shadrach, Meshach, and Abed-Nego. These Jewish men forced to serve the Babylonian King Nebuchadnezzar were put in a tight spot. The king builds a statue and decrees all should bow down to it. The Chaldeans saw this as an opportunity to get rid of the Jews, telling the king that Shadrach, Meshach, and Abed-Nego disobeyed his decree. When faced with the choice of bowing down to the king or being thrown into the fiery furnace, they chose to stand for God and into the fiery furnace they were thrown! Even as they made that choice, I imagine they were praying their hardest! But God controlled the situation, never leaving them and protecting them in the fire. *"Then King*

Nebuchadnezzar was astonished; and he rose in haste and spoke, saying to his counselors, "Did we not cast three men bound into the midst of the fire?" They answered and said to the king, "True, O king." "Look!" he answered, "I see four men loose, walking in the midst of the fire; and they are not hurt, and the form of the fourth is like the Son of God," Daniel 3:24-25. The king and his counselors may have been surprised at this but God was prepared and protected His followers.

As a result of their choice to stand for God, God received the glory. *"Nebuchadnezzar spoke, saying, "Blessed be the God of Shadrach, Meshach, and Abed-Nego, who sent His Angel and delivered His servants who trusted in Him, and they have frustrated the king's word, and yielded their bodies, that they should not serve nor worship any god except their own God! Therefore, I make a decree that any people, nation, or language which speaks anything amiss against the God of Shadrach, Meshach, and Abed-Nego shall be cut in pieces, and their houses shall be made an ash heap; because there is no other God who can deliver like this,"* Daniel 3:28-29.

Our loving God is never surprised and always prepared for everything. Let's all turn to God in every situation, praying, trusting, and watching as He does what only He can do – the impossible!

REFLECTION

- What does Ephesians 4:6 say to you about God's abilities?

- What surprises have you had in your life, good or bad? How did it turn out? Was God's sovereignty evident in the outcome?

- Are you currently facing any surprises in your life? How can the knowledge of God's sovereignty help?

We can trust that God is able to handle
any situation because God is sovereign
and never surprised.

FAITH FOCUS

God is sovereign and never surprised.

"One God and Father of all,
who is above all,
and through all, and in you all,"

Ephesians 4:6

PRAYER

Heavenly Father, write this Scripture on my heart as I read it out loud and write it in my Faith Notebook.

Heavenly Father, help me to see evidence of this Scripture today.

Record what you see, hear, or experience today that shows evidence of this Scripture.

DAY FIVE

"And the Lord passed by before him, and proclaimed, The LORD, The Lord God, merciful and gracious, longsuffering, and abounding in goodness and truth."

Exodus 34:6

I WENT THE WRONG WAY!

Bumping along the rutted dirt road, you begin to wonder if the GPS is leading you to the correct destination when it suddenly stops working. Oh Noooo! There must not be a signal in this place! Frustrated but determined to arrive at your destination, you turn several times as new roads pop up. After a while, you realize you are lost. You keep looking for a different road to turn onto, hoping that you can change your destination, but none are in sight. As you look around at the secluded area, you wonder, "Where am I? This can't be right! All the roads I turned onto were definitely wrong for me to wind up here! Now there is no doubt that I am lost! Please, can somebody help me find a way out!"

Has your GPS ever led you to the wrong destination? Or have you ever taken a wrong turn and felt lost hoping someone would help you find your way? Don't we all do that at one time or another as we make decisions on which road to take in life? What happens when we take the wrong road in life, one that doesn't include God's path for us? Does God just throw up His hands and say forget them?

Let's look at the Israelite slaves in Egypt. In Exodus chapters 7-12, we find the story of God rescuing the Israelites from slavery in Egypt. I would imagine that after 430 years of slavery (Exodus 12:40), they felt lost. Just like the driver looking for a different road to change his destination, they too kept looking for a way to alter their destination in life.

They, like the lost driver, cried out for help, and God heeded the Israelites cry, (Exodus 2:23-25). Why would God heed their cry? Were they all on the road God had for them, listening to God and following His commands? Impossible! Out of over 600,000 (Exodus 12:37-38) men plus women and children, there had to be a number of them who took a wrong turn in life. Do you think every last one of them even believed in God? Even after witnessing God's miracles in Egypt, there were probably many who did not believe in God but followed God's command to leave Egypt as a way to escape slavery. Yet, we find no evidence that God checked their motives. Nor did He segregate those who believed from those who didn't. He heard their cry and saved them all from the bondage of slavery. Not only that, but God healed them all as not one of them was feeble when they left," (Psalm 105:37).

Why would God do that? Because God in His great love for us is merciful, *"But God, who is rich in mercy, because of his great love with which He loved us,"* Ephesians 2:4. *"Mercy"* in Strong's Greek #1656, is defined as compassion. Our compassionate God sees our sufferings and wants to bring us out of bondage to follow His road of blessings. At one time or another, we may all have turned down a path that put us in bondage to fear, addiction, unforgiveness, idols, or doubt, to name a few. For those who don't believe in Jesus, there is the bondage of unbelief that leads many to perish. It doesn't matter how long we have been driving down the wrong road, God's desire is to rescue us all, *"The Lord is not slack concerning His promise, as some count slackness; but is longsuffering toward us, not willing that any should perish, but that all should come to repentance,"* 2 Peter 3:9. When we go down the wrong road, God in His mercy is waiting for our cry for help so that He can rescue us all.

REFLECTION

- What does the story of the Israelites tell you about God's mercy?

- What wrong turns have you taken and why?

- Do you believe God's mercy extends to you?

- Describe what Ephesians 2:4 and 2 Peter 3:9 says about God's mercy for you.

We can trust that God is willing and able
to reach out to us no matter what road we are on
because God is merciful.

FAITH FOCUS

God is merciful because He loves us so much.

"And the Lord passed by before him, and proclaimed,
The LORD, The Lord God, merciful and gracious,
longsuffering, and abounding in goodness and truth,"
Exodus 34:6

PRAYER

Heavenly Father, write this Scripture on my heart as I read it out loud and write it in my Faith Notebook.

Heavenly Father, help me to see evidence of this Scripture today.

Record what you see, hear, or experience today
that shows evidence of this Scripture.

DAY SIX

"Ah, Lord God! Behold,

You have made the heavens and the earth by Your great power and outstretched arm. There is nothing too hard for You."

Jeremiah 32:17

I NEED A MIRACLE!

A smile crosses your face as you view the crystal blue sky, sparkling water, and snowcapped mountains outside your window. After days of soaking rain, you can finally go on your much-awaited hike. Quickly lacing up your hiking boots, you set out. Squish, squish, squish, your shoes noisily sound as you walk on the saturated ground. With each step that you take, your shoes seem to disappear as they turn brown with the mud seeping onto your shoes. The further you walk, the more difficult it becomes to remove your shoes from the mud until they are so entrenched that you can't move them at all! You can't even pull your feet out of your shoes! No one is around, the sun is quickly setting, and the temperature is rapidly dropping! "Help, I am trapped! I can't escape the mud!" you shout. When no one responds, all you can think of is, God, I need a miracle!

Miracles! God's specialty. All through the Scriptures, we see God working miracles. Let's look again at the Israelites. Take the example of the Israelites at the Red Sea, Exodus 14:1-31. After 430 years as slaves, Pharaoh releases the Israelites to leave Egypt freely. But soon Pharaoh is sorry that he has let the slaves go, and with his army of 600 chariots, he goes after the Israelites to enslave them again. Hearing the Israelites were camped by the Red Sea, the Egyptians knew that they were trapped. There was no way for the Israelites to escape them now.

But just like they did in the land of Egypt, the Egyptians forgot the power of God. In a situation with seemingly insurmountable odds, only God could help the Israelites. Amid the Israelites' fear and doubt, God showed His power again and performed a miracle. BAM! In an instant, the Lord made a dry path through the Red Sea onto the other side. Just imagine the faith that it took for the Israelites to step into the Red Sea and take the long journey across.

Just imagine their fear that the walls of water would collapse, the shouts as they ran to escape the Egyptians and their surprise that the path was so dry that their shoes, nor flocks, got stuck in the mud!

What about what they saw? It would be like a visit to the North Carolina aquarium that takes you down a path with glass walls on either side where you can view the fish, sharks, and other sea life beside you. But I guess the Israelites must have been in too much of a hurry to take in the view. Flanked by approximately 300 foot walls of water[7] they hustled safely to the other side. With over 600,000 men plus women and children, this would not have been a sprint because they were loaded down with their flocks and all the goodies the Lord had given them from the Egyptians, Exodus 12:32,35-36.

But with all that God had done, He was not finished yet. Once the Israelites had all made it to the other side of the Red Sea, BAM! God returns the sea to normal, and it envelopes every single Egyptian in it, providing dinner for the fishes. So, God not only sets the Israelites free from their bondage as slaves, gives them an abundance of provision and brings them to safety, He also destroys the Egyptians so that they cannot continue to try to harm the Israelites. Now that's what I call a miracle!

Whenever we come against seemingly insurmountable odds, let's remember what our loving God has done and have faith that God can still be victorious no matter what we see or hear. *"Ah, Lord God! Behold, You have made the heavens and the earth by Your great power and outstretched arm. There is nothing too hard for You,"* Jeremiah 32:17

REFLECTION

- What did God do for the Israelites in Exodus chapter 14 that showed His power?

[7] TrueDiscoveries.com

- When have you been stuck in the mud with an internal or external struggle? How did God help you get out?
- Do you believe that God is still able to demonstrate that kind of power today? Why or why not? Does your belief align with Jeremiah 32:17?

Since God never changes, we can trust that nothing is too hard for God because His power enables Him to do the impossible.

FAITH FOCUS

God is powerful.

"Ah, Lord God! Behold, You have made the heavens and the earth by Your great power and outstretched arm. There is nothing too hard for You,"

Jeremiah 32:17

PRAYER

Heavenly Father, write this Scripture on my heart as I read it out loud and write it in my Faith Notebook.

Heavenly Father, help me to see evidence of this Scripture today.

Record what you see, hear, or experience today that shows evidence of this Scripture.

ENRICHMENT STEP 1
Day 1-6

1. So that you can literally feel and understand that faith in God requires us to trust in the love and capability of God to guide us through any situation, duplicate the obstacle course in Step 1, 'God is Trustworthy and Able' on Page 1 by doing the steps below.

For this exercise you will need two partners, a blind fold, and a soft obstacle course.

- Select two partners who love you; one whose abilities you trust to guide you and one who is more challenged in guiding you.

- Have the partners create an obstacle course. Safety first! Be sure it is in a very safe environment where they cannot run into anything that will harm them!

- Have one partner blindfold you and bring you to the obstacle course.

- Have one partner verbally guide you through the course.

- Have the partners make a few changes to the course and let the second partner repeat the activity.

At the end of the activity answer these questions;

- How did you feel when the capable partner guided you through the course?

- How did you feel when the challenged partner guided you through the course?

- At the end of the activity did you feel either partner no longer loved you?

- Did you feel both partners had your best interest at heart?

Remember that as we run the race of life, we need to trust that God loves us, has our best interest at heart and is capable of guiding us so that we avoid or overcome any obstacles we will ever face.

27

2. To keep God's Word before our eyes and deeply implant it in our hearts, select at least one verse from Day 1-6 to memorize and keep in front of you.

Write the verse on an index card and tape it on your bathroom mirror. Each time you face the mirror, read the verse out loud.

"Therefore you shall lay up
these words of mine in your heart and in your soul,
and bind them as a sign on your hand,
and they shall be as frontlets between your eyes."
Deuteronomy 11:18

STEP 2
GOD'S LOVE

There are so many people, thinks the child. "Are we really going in there?" he asks with a shaky voice. His eyes grow wide as he surveys the crowded scene. You feel his tiny hand slip into yours. He tightly holds on but keeps pace with you as you enter the crowd because he trusts you to take care of him. Why? Because he knows that you love him.

We, like children, sometimes experience a little fear as we anticipate the worst when we walk into a crowded situation. Who can blame anyone for feeling that way when we live in violent times. So, what should we do to squelch our fears? No matter what the situation, we can act in the opposite of fear, which is faith, *"For we walk by faith, not by sight,"* 2 Corinthians 5:7. While fear anticipates the worse, faith expects God's outcome because we trust that He will be victorious and act in our best interest. Faith allows us to trust as a child and slip our hand into our loving God's, tightly holding on as we enter any situation.

So how do we build a faith that will allow us to do that? By building a relationship with a foundation of love. As we are assured how much God loves us, then we trust that He will act in our best interest.

Part of that assurance comes from understanding and putting the truth of His Scriptures and His love in our hearts and minds.

For the next 7 days, (Days 7-13), our journey will be just that, to better understand and implant God's love in our hearts and minds. This is the next step in building our faith.

Daily Scripture Reading
Allows You To
Grow Your Faith
One Day at a Time

DAY SEVEN

"For the LORD your God is God of gods and Lord of lords,

the great God,

mighty and awesome, who shows no partiality nor takes a bribe."

Deuteronomy 10:17

I PICK YOU!

John, Frank, and Sally stood nervously side by side. "I pick John," said the red team captain. With a big smile, John runs to join the red team. With wide-eyed anticipation, Frank and Sally look at the blue team captain, hoping to be picked next. "I pick Sally," said the blue team captain. With a sigh of relief, Sally runs to join the blue team. "Frank," said his teacher, "that means you are on the red team." The last one picked, thought Frank as he slowly shuffled along, why did I have to be the last one? Doesn't anybody like me?

Whether it's a sport or any other competition, no one likes to be picked last. It makes us feel unloved and inferior even before the competition begins. All of us have experienced being picked last for a team where we were not the best and the brightest. We assume since humans do that, God also favors the best and the brightest. But God has no favorites. He treats all of us the same, *"For the LORD your God is God of gods and Lord of lords, the great God, mighty and awesome, who shows no partiality nor takes a bribe,"* Deuteronomy 10:17.

God doesn't look for perfection, social standing, wealth, the best in their field, or the brightest. He doesn't care what we look like or how many friends we have. God is not partial. He loves us all and desires that we all come to Him no matter who we are or what we have done, *"The Lord is not slack concerning His promise, as some count slackness; but is longsuffering toward us, not willing that any should perish, but that all should come to repentance,"* 2 Peter 3:9.

God's love for us is not like the love of a flawed human, but His love for us is perfect, impartial, and vast beyond our imagination. It doesn't matter who we are or what we have done, God still loves us all. God's love for us is:

Unconditional – *"This is love: not that we loved God, but that He loved us and sent His Son as an atoning sacrifice for our sin."* 1 John 4:10. (NIV)

Inseparable – *"For I am persuaded that neither death nor life, nor angels, nor principalities, nor power, nor things present nor things to come, nor height, nor depth, nor any other creature shall be able to separate us from the love of God which is in Christ Jesus our Lord,"* Romans 8:38-39.

Pure –*"... God is love,"* 1 John 4:8.

Everlasting – *"The Lord has appeared of old to me saying, Yes, I have loved you with an everlasting love; therefore, with lovingkindness I have drawn you,"* Jeremiah 31:3.

Great –*"But God, who is rich in mercy, for His great love wherein He loved us,"* Ephesians 2:4.

Vast – *"That Christ may dwell in your hearts by faith; that you, being rooted and grounded in love, may be able to comprehend with all saints what is the width and length, and depth and height – to know the love of Christ which passes knowledge; that you might be filled with all the fullness of God,"* Ephesians. 3:17-19.

So next time we need a little love, let's reach out to God and remember how very much our God loves each and every one of us – no matter who we are or what we have done.

REFLECTION

- Have you ever felt unaccepted? Describe the situation and why you felt that way.

- Describe a time when you felt accepted and loved and why you felt that way.

- How does your belief in God's love for you compare to either of those situations?

- Rewrite Deuteronomy 10:17 in your own words. Does your belief in God's love and acceptance of you match the Scripture?

God loves me no matter who I am
because God is not partial.

FAITH FOCUS

God chooses to love me just the way I am

"For the LORD your God is
God of gods and Lord of lords,
the great God, mighty and awesome,
who shows no partiality nor takes a bribe,"

Deuteronomy 10:17

PRAYER

Heavenly Father, write this Scripture on my heart as I read it out loud and write it in my Faith Notebook.

Heavenly Father, help me to see evidence of this Scripture today.

Record what you see, hear, or experience today
that shows evidence of this Scripture.

DAY EIGHT

"*This is love: not that we loved God, but that He loved us and sent His Son as an atoning sacrifice for our sins.*"

1 John 4:10 NIV

NO STRINGS ATTACHED!

Conditions! Have you ever heard these statements? IF you are good, THEN you will get ice cream. IF you do your homework, THEN, you can watch TV. IF you pass your driver's test, THEN you can get your license. IF you are qualified, THEN you can get a job interview. IF you earn enough money, THEN you can get a mortgage loan. Conditions! Conditions! Conditions! It seems there are always strings attached to obtaining our desires!

All through life, we are faced with conditional situations. IF we meet particular behavior, performance, experience, or financial standards, THEN we may have the opportunity to obtain our desires. But there is one unconditional thing. Getting it does not require we behave a certain way. It does not require that we meet any performance expectations. We do not have to have any experience, nor do we need to meet any financial standards. We can't earn it, and we don't have to reciprocate it. We can ignore it. We can refuse it. But it is still there, unconditional and freely given. What is it? It is God's unconditional love. *"This is love: not that we loved God, but that He loved us and sent His Son as an atoning sacrifice for our sins,"* 1 John 4:10. (NIV)

Even if we hate the giver, God's love is given unconditionally, with no strings attached. And no matter who we are, what we do, or how much we push God away, God still loves us. *"For I am persuaded that neither death nor life, nor angels nor principalities nor powers, nor things present nor things to come, nor height nor depth, nor any other created thing, shall be able to separate us from the love of God which is in Christ Jesus our Lord,"* Romans 8:38-39. God's love is a gift freely given, always available with no strings attached for ALL of us!

REFLECTION

- Have you ever received a gift given with no strings attached, but given just because the person cared about you? If so, how did that make you feel when you received it?

- Do you feel the same way about receiving God's love? Why or why not?

- Do you feel you are required to behave or perform a certain way in order to receive God's love? Be specific.

- According to 1 John 4:10, what requirements does God place on us to receive His love?

God loves me no matter what,
even when I don't love Him

FAITH FOCUS

God's love for me is unconditional,
no strings attached!

*"This is love: not that we loved God,
but that He loved us and sent His Son
as an atoning sacrifice for our sins,"*

1 John 4:10 (NIV)

PRAYER

> Heavenly Father, write this Scripture on my heart as I read it out loud and write it in my Faith Notebook.
>
> Heavenly Father, help me to see evidence of this Scripture today.

Record what you see, hear, or experience today
that shows evidence of this Scripture.

Daily Scripture Reading
Allows You To
Grow Your Faith
One Day at a Time

DAY NINE

"For I am persuaded that neither death nor life, nor angels nor principalities nor powers, nor things present nor things to come, nor height nor depth, nor any other created thing, shall be able to separate us from the love of God which is in Christ Jesus our Lord,"

Romans 8:38-39

YOU CAN"T HIDE!

You yell, "1,2, 3, 4, 5, 6, 7, 8, 9, 10! Ready or not, here I come!" Silently you creep up to the wide oak tree, hoping to find someone to tag. Laughing, your friend jumps from behind the tree and runs just out of your reach to the safety of home base. With determination, you continue your search. Spying the top of a red shoe peaking out beneath the hedges, you carefully approach. All of a sudden, not one but several friends rush out from the hedges to try to escape your tag. But one is a little too slow. You tag him and excitedly exclaim, "You're it!"

Playing tag, we hope to hide well enough that we can safely make it to base before being tagged "it." But no matter where we hide and no matter where we run, fast or slow, there is always someone who knows where we are and can tag us – God. Similarly, God has implanted the most sophisticated GPS into our hearts so that He knows where we are and can tag us with His love anytime, anywhere. Satellite systems may go down so people can't be tracked. Large oak trees and hedges can be so full of leaves that we aren't exposed. We can hide in a cave or even the bottom of the ocean. It doesn't matter where we are, God in His abounding, merciful love is with us. We can break all of the 10 Commandments, curse like a sailor, and commit a felony, but God will still love us. There is nothing we can do, or there is nowhere we can go that will separate us from God's love or take us beyond God's reach, *"For I am persuaded that neither death nor life, nor angels nor principalities nor powers, nor things present nor things to come, nor height nor depth, nor any other created thing, shall be able to separate us from the love of God which is in Christ Jesus our Lord,"* Romans 8:38-39.

Next time we feel alone, discouraged, or forgotten, let's remember our God who knows our hearts, sees us wherever we are, and still wants to tag us with His love. Because there is nothing we can do or nowhere we can go that can separate us from His abounding, merciful love.

REFLECTION

- Have you ever cared about someone but something was said or done that caused a separation and loss of love in the relationship? Describe the situation.

- Write Romans 8:38-39 in your own words.

- According to Romans 8:38-39, can any word or action on your part end God's love for you? Is there anywhere you can go to escape God's love for you?

> God sees you as you are and wherever you are
> yet there is nothing you can do to escape
> God's love for you.

FAITH FOCUS

There is nowhere I can hide from God's love for me

"For I am persuaded that neither death nor life, nor angels nor principalities nor powers, nor things present nor things to come, nor height nor depth, nor any other created thing, shall be able to separate us from the love of God which is in Christ Jesus our Lord,"

Romans 8:38-39

PRAYER

Heavenly Father, write this Scripture on my heart as I read it out loud and write it in my Faith Notebook.

Heavenly Father, help me to see evidence of this Scripture today.

Record what you see, hear, or experience today
that shows evidence of this Scripture.

Daily Scripture Reading
Allows You To
Grow Your Faith
One Day at a Time

DAY TEN

"*God is love.*"

1 John 4:8

FILTERED WATER PLEASE!

The canteen is empty! Your throat is parched D-R-Y! It is so hot that even the shade of the forest gives little relief from the heat. The hike up the mountain required more water than you anticipated, and now you are really, really thirsty. It may be your imagination, but you hear the sound of a bathtub running. You are sure you are hallucinating, but you follow the sound. Oh, thank the Lord, a stream! Approaching cautiously (in case there are any thirsty bears) you find crystal clear water cascading over the rocks. You plunge your hands in the stream and gulp up the wonderfully pure-tasting water.

Lumbering down the mountain, you follow the stream so you can drink from it as needed. After a couple of miles, you see the stream feeds into a pond. However, you notice the pond's water is not as clear as the stream at the top of the mountain. The few houses in the area must have caused some pollution which deters you from taking a drink. On the other side of the pond, a stream runs down the mountain. From there, the water flows into a lake in the valley. The lake situated in a very populated area is obviously polluted. You need a drink, but wait until you get to the store to purchase some pure, filtered water.

Like God created pure water at the top of the mountain, God created pure love. But, man's thoughts have polluted God's love. Man's polluted thoughts have said that God cannot love me because I have made too many mistakes. But God's pure love says, *"For I am persuaded that neither death nor life, nor angels nor principalities nor powers, nor things present nor things to come, nor height nor depth, nor any other created thing, shall be able to separate us from the love of God which is in Christ Jesus our Lord,"* Romans 8:38-39.

Man's polluted thoughts have said that God cannot love me because I don't love Him. But, God's pure love says, *"This is love: not that we loved God, but that He loved us and sent His Son as an atoning sacrifice for our sin,"* 1 John 4:10. (NIV)

Man's polluted thoughts have said that I am so far away from God that He could never love me. But God's pure love says God's love is so vast that it reaches you wherever you are, *"That Christ may dwell in your hearts through faith; that you, being rooted and grounded in love, may be able to comprehend with all the saints what is the width and length and depth and height – to know the love of Christ which passes knowledge; that you may be filled with all the fullness of God,"* Ephesians 3:17-19.

Man's polluted thoughts have said that God cannot love me because I don't preach, I'm not in the choir, and I don't teach so I am unimportant. But God's pure love says that you are significant. *"But the very hairs of your head are all numbered. Do not fear therefore; you are of more value than many sparrows,"* Luke 12:7.

God's pure love says that no matter where you are or what you have done, He will never stop loving you. *"The Lord has appeared of old to me, saying: "Yes, I have loved you with an everlasting love; Therefore, with lovingkindness I have drawn you,"* Jeremiah 31:3.

Let's filter man's pollution from our thoughts and receive the refreshment of God's pure, life-giving love.

REFLECTION

- What are some mistakes you have made? Do you feel those mistakes prohibit God from loving you?
- Using the verses above, identify 5 characteristics of God's love for you.
- Reflecting on God's characteristics of love for you, what polluted thoughts do you need to change about God's love for you?

God still loves me no matter
what I think about Him

FAITH FOCUS

God's love for me is pure

"God is love,"
1 John 4:8

PRAYER

Heavenly Father, write this Scripture on my heart as I read it out loud and write it in my Faith Notebook.

Heavenly Father, help me to see evidence of this Scripture today.

Record what you see, hear, or experience today
that shows evidence of this Scripture.

DAY ELEVEN

"The LORD has appeared
of old to me, saying:

"Yes, I have loved you
with an everlasting love,

Therefore with
lovingkindness I have
drawn you."

Jeremiah 31:3

LIFETIME WARRANTY!

"Oh, no! Look at all this water!" The laundry room floor looks like a little pond from the leaking washing machine. You slosh through the water to turn off the washer and spend the next 30 minutes mopping and dumping buckets of water. Now, you have to get it fixed. You search for the warranty. When does the warranty expire on it? You guessed it! It expired two days ago! "Uggggh!" It's so frustrating!! Why do items break just after the warranty expires? It's like the manufacturer made it last just long enough so that they would not have to replace the broken part. Of course, that is not true. However, what is true is that the goal of the manufacturer is to make a profit, so they usually offer short warranties as they prefer not to repair or replace products because it affects their profits. Wouldn't it be nice if all products came with lifetime warranties?

Compared to the number of products available on the market, the number of products that have a lifetime warranty is minuscule. Those products can still break, but at least the manufacturer promises that they will replace or repair them, as long as the manufacturer honestly stands behind their warranty and they stay in business.

But how about a warranty that we not only know we can count on, but that will last past our lifetime? Yes, there is one, the guarantee or promise of the everlasting love of God. God is eternal, so He will never ever go out of business; *The LORD shall reign forever and ever,"* Exodus 15:18. God will always stand behind His warranty of love because He cannot lie, *"God is not a man, that He should lie, nor a son of man, that He should repent. Has He said, and will He not do? Or has He spoken, and will He not make it good?"* Numbers 23:19. God's warranty of love is everlasting. It extends into eternity. And if our relationship with God needs to be repaired, we profit because in His great love for us, His desire is always to fix it with His lovingkindness, *"The LORD has appeared of old to me, saying: "Yes, I have loved you with an everlasting love; Therefore, with lovingkindness I have drawn you,"* Jeremiah 31:3. The warranty for God's love is provided by a faithful, honest God who stands behind His Creation. His warranty of love never expires going beyond our lifetime into eternity. Now that's a warranty you can count on!

REFLECTION

- Do you feel your relationship with God is broken? If so, why?

- If you asked God to repair it, how do you feel God would react? Does your belief align with Deuteronomy 10:17 and 2 Peter 3:9, (hint Day 7)?

- According to Jeremiah 31:3, describe how God would draw you back to Him.

- According to Jeremiah 31:3, is there an expiration date on God's love for you?

God is always there for us
extending His hand in a love
that will never expire

FAITH FOCUS

God's love for me will never end!

"The LORD has appeared of old to me, saying:
"Yes, I have loved you with an everlasting love;
Therefore with lovingkindness I have drawn you,"

Jeremiah 31:3

PRAYER

Heavenly Father, write this Scripture on my heart as I read it out loud and write it in my Faith Notebook.

Heavenly Father, help me to see evidence of this Scripture today.

Record what you see, hear, or experience today that shows evidence of this Scripture.

DAY TWELVE

*"But God,
who is rich in mercy
for His great love
wherein He loved us."*

Ephesians 2:4

24/7!

It's 12:01 a.m. Ding! Facebook says today is Ginger's birthday. At 3:00 a.m., Da, da, da, da! your phone receives a text message while you are asleep. Riiiinnnggg! It's 2:00 p.m., and your computer has an email. At 6:30 p.m., you walk down the grocery aisle hearing, Clang! Clang! Clang! You reach in your pocket to answer your phone. Our technology now is so advanced that it allows us to be reached 24/7, wherever we are. Well, wherever they have wireless service and our battery is not dead.

I guess that makes God the perfect technology because God is accessible 24/7, even when there is no wireless service! God's love for us is so great that He answers us at the perfect time and in a way that is always perfect for us. (2 Samuel 22:31) No matter when we call or where we are, God will answer. It doesn't matter if it's 3:00 a.m. or if we have just made the biggest mistake of our lives, God is there with His abundant mercy and great love. *"But God, who is rich in mercy for His great love wherein He loved us,"* Ephesians 2:4. Why? Because His love is unconditional, *"This is love: not that we loved God, but that He loved us and sent His Son as an atoning sacrifice for our sin."* 1 John 4:10. (NIV)

So, let's all reach out to God, who does not need a battery or wireless service to answer us and who is always available 24/7. *"Behold, He who keeps Israel shall neither slumber nor sleep,"* Psalm 121:4.

REFLECTION

- Has there been a time when you needed God? Describe where you were, how you reached out to God and how God communicated with you.

- What are some ways God can communicate with us? (hint; John 14:26, Matthew 1:20, Acts 18:9, 2 Timothy 3:16, Acts 9:4-5, Deuteronomy 18:18, Leviticus 1:2)

- What does Psalm 121:4 mean to you?

God in His love for us is always available

FAITH FOCUS

God's love for me is so great
that He makes Himself available 24/7!

*"But God, who is rich in mercy for
His great love wherein He loved us,"*

Ephesians 2:4.

PRAYER

Heavenly Father, write this Scripture on my heart as I read it out loud and write it in my Faith Notebook.

Heavenly Father, help me to see evidence of this Scripture today.

Record what you see, hear, or experience today
that shows evidence of this Scripture.

Daily Scripture Reading
Allows You To
Grow Your Faith
One Day at a Time

DAY THIRTEEN

"That Christ may dwell in your hearts through faith, that you, being rooted and grounded in love, may be able to comprehend with all the saints what is the width and length and depth and height— to know the love of Christ which passes knowledge, that you may be filled with all the fullness of God. Ephesians 3:17-19

HOW BIG IS BIG!

Have you ever been to the Grand Canyon? I have only seen photos, which probably do not do it justice. Even in pictures, you can see that the canyon is immense! It is 277 miles long, up to 18 miles wide and over a mile deep – 6, 093 ft. to be exact. If you think that is big, how about the Mariana Trench in the Pacific Ocean? This trench is the deepest in the world at 36, 070 feet deep! Also found on an island, in where else but the Pacific, is the highest mountain in the world, Mauna Kea. When measured from its' underwater base, Mauna Kea is 33,474 ft. high. And let's not forget the longest river in the world, measuring 4,345 miles, the Amazon River runs not just through one, but through several countries. It also holds the title of the widest river in the world at 202 miles wide at its' estuary.[8] I don't know about you, but I cannot begin to comprehend the width, length, depth, or height of these places!

If we can't comprehend the immense size of these places that we can see, how can we comprehend the tremendous nature of God's love for us? As the Scripture says, *"That Christ may dwell in your hearts through faith; that you, being rooted and grounded in love, may be able to comprehend with all the saints what is the width and length and depth and height— to know the love of Christ which passes knowledge; that you may be filled with all the fullness of God,"* Ephesians 3:17-19.

God created each of these beautiful wonders; the Grand Canyon, Mauna Kea, the Amazon River, and the Mariana Trench. Only someone who loves us would take the time to create such magnificent wonders for us to see. Only someone who is larger than these wonders could have a love for us that is larger than anything we can see. Only someone who has such a vast love for us would always be there when we call Him, whenever we need

[8] All facts regarding miles, feet, etc. from Wikipedia.com

Him, no matter where we are. Like the 1967 song, *Ain't No Mountain High Enough* says, "If you need me, call me, no matter where you are, no matter how far, don't worry, baby. Just call my name, I'll be there in a hurry, you don't have to worry. Cause baby there ain't no mountain high enough, Ain't no valley low enough, Ain't no river wide enough, To keep me from getting to you babe.[9]"

God's love for us is so vast. It is higher than the highest mountain, wider than the broadest river, and His power enables Him to reach us when we call, no matter where we are because we are never far from His hand.

REFLECTION

- Describe how much you feel God loves you.

- In your own words, describe what Ephesians 3:17 is saying about God's love for you.

- Think about the person whom you love the most. How does your love for that person compare to God's love for you in Ephesians 3:17? Can God's love for you be any less than our human love?

God's love for us is so vast

it is greater than anything we can see

FAITH FOCUS

God's love for me is vast

*"That Christ may dwell in your hearts through faith;
that you, being rooted and grounded in love,
may be able to comprehend with all the saints what is the width
and length and depth and height—to know
the love of Christ which passes knowledge;
that you may be filled with all the fullness of God,"*

Ephesians 3:17-19

[9] Nickolas Ashford & Valerie Simpson

PRAYER

Heavenly Father, write this Scripture on my heart as I read it out loud and write it in my Faith Notebook.

Heavenly Father, help me to see evidence of this Scripture today.

Record what you see, hear, or experience today that shows evidence of this Scripture.

ENRICHMENT STEP 2
Day 7-13

1. To plant God's love for us deeper into our hearts, we will look at labels we place on ourselves. We label ourselves with descriptions of who we are, what we look like, etc. For these and numerous other reasons, we often label ourselves unlovable causing ourselves to feel God won't love us. Others label us as well and we believe the labels they have given us, good or bad. As you have read how very much our heavenly God loves you, I pray you have been able to remove some of those unlovable labels and receive His great love for you. Let's examine any remaining unlovable labels you have so that you can plant more of God's love for you into your heart.

For this exercise you will need a pen, a mirror and some sticky notes or labels.

- Pray about any labels you may still hold onto that make you feel unlovable. As those labels come to mind, write them on a sticky note or label.

- On separate labels, write Scripture verses that say that God loves you just the way you are. You may use the Scriptures from this section of the book, research your own or refer to some examples below.

- Stick each unlovable label you wrote on your chest and stand in front of a mirror.

- Once all unlovable labels are on your chest, remove them one at a time and replace them with the Scripture labels speaking as follows:

  - God has not made me (fill in your unlovable label).

  - God has made me (read your Scripture).

- When you are finished, throw away the unlovable labels and retain the Scriptures somewhere you can reference them if unlovable thoughts return.

Unlovable label	God's Truthful Label
Rejected	**Accepted in the Beloved** Ephesians 1:5-6 *Having predestined us to adoption as sons by Jesus Christ to Himself, according to the good pleasure of His will, to the praise of the glory of His grace, by which He made us accepted in the Beloved.*
Ugly	**Fearfully and Wonderfully Made** Psalm 139:14 *I will praise You, for I am fearfully and wonderfully made; Marvelous are Your works, And that my soul knows very well.* (Ephesians 2:10)
Friendless, Alone, Forgettable	**God is Always With Us & Will Not Forget Us** Isaiah 49:15-16 *Can a woman forget her nursing child, And not have compassion on the son of her womb? Surely they may forget, Yet I will not forget you. See, I have inscribed you on the palms of My hands; Your walls are continually before Me.* (Deuteronomy 31:6)
Unworthy	**Righteousness of God** 2 Corinthians 5:21 *For He made Him who knew no sin to be sin for us, that we might become the righteousness of God in Him.* (1 John 1:9)
Rejected by our family	**Part of God's Family** Psalm 27:10 *When my father and my mother forsake me, Then the Lord will take care of me.* (1 John 3:1, John 1:12)

2. Once again, to keep God's Word before our eyes and deeply implanted in our hearts, select at least one verse from Day 7-13 to memorize and keep in front of you.

Write the verse on an index card and tape it on your refrigerator. Each time you reach into the refrigerator, read the verse out loud.

Your words were found, and I ate them, And Your word was to me the joy and rejoicing of my heart; For I am called by Your name, O Lord God of hosts. Jeremiah 15:16

STEP 3
FAITH

"Hello! Anybody home?" you call as you lay your keys on the table. Hearing no reply, you shuffle wearily to the kitchen and open the refrigerator. Umm, nobody's home, so I'll just have a bowl of cereal. Seeing two full cartons of milk, you have faith that there will be plenty of milk for breakfast. After cleaning up, you turn off all of the house lights and go to bed. You sleep peacefully, having faith that nothing will change during the night.

It is easy to have faith when we see the evidence of something. Faith that whatever we saw when we went to bed will be unchanged in the morning. Faith that our keys will still be on the table, faith that the house lights will still be off and faith that the milk carton will still be full. Unless you have a house full of teenagers, then all bets are off – everything can change! But you get the idea.

If we can see something, is that really faith? Faith, what is it? The Scriptures define it in Hebrews 11:1, *"Now faith is the substance of things hoped for, the evidence of things not seen."* This is not hoped for like we use it where there is a 50/50 chance it will happen. Hoped for means to "trust.[10]" Substance means "confidence.[11]" To restate it with those definitions, it says, 'Now faith is the confidence for things trusted for, the evidence of things not seen.' So true faith is the expectation of something we haven't yet seen.

[10] Strong's Concordance, Greek #1679
[11] Strong's Concordance, Greek #5287

We have taken the first two foundational steps in building our faith by developing more trust in God as we learned about God's trustworthiness, abilities, and love. For Days 14 – 31, let's look at increasing our faith and walking in it.

"But he who received seed on the good ground is he who hears the word and understands it, who indeed bears fruit and produces: some a hundredfold, some sixty, some thirty."

Matthew 13: 23

GROW YOUR GARDEN!

The vivid splashes of color on the rack catch your eye as you enter the garden shop. Oh, how beautiful you think as you examine the rows of seed packages. Dreamily you imagine a garden full of all of the beautiful flowers you see. Sighing, you realize that your gardening skills would not produce the garden you envision. Neither would mine. However, I do know at least the basics. Things needed to grow a plant are good soil, water, and light. Without these, all we would get are weeds and dead plants. Why are we talking about plants? Remember the mustard seed Jesus compared to faith? *"Truly I tell you, if you have faith as small as a mustard seed, you can say to this mountain, 'Move from here to there,' and it will move. Nothing will be impossible for you,"* Matthew 17:20.

The mustard seed may start out small, but when planted in good ground and given water and light, it can grow into a plant that is large, strong, and provides shelter. *"Again he said, "What shall we say the kingdom of God is like, or what parable shall we use to describe it? 31 It is like a mustard seed, which is the smallest of all seeds on earth. 32 Yet when planted, it grows and becomes the largest of all garden plants, with such big branches that the birds can perch in its shade,"* Mark 4:30-32. NIV

We can grow our faith the same way we grow that tiny mustard seed with:

1. **Good Ground** – *"But he who received seed on the good ground is he who hears the **word** and understands it, who indeed bears fruit and produces: some a hundredfold, some sixty, some thirty,"* Matthew 13: 23.

2. **Water** – *"That He might sanctify and cleanse her with the washing of water by the **word**,"* Ephesians 5:26.

3. **Light** – *"Your **word** is a lamp to my feet, and a light to my path,"* Psalm 119:105.

Notice these three things have one thing in common, God's Word. Because God loves us, He has given us His Word to grow our faith and give us the answers we seek on healing, finances, direction, or anything else. Together let's all grow our faith with God's Word by:

- Reading and listening to it (Romans 10:17)
- Seeking to understand it (Matthew 13:23)
- Allowing it to cleanse us (Ephesians 5:26)
- Letting it guide us (Psalm 119:105)

If our tiny mustard seed faith can do the impossible, just imagine how the Lord can use us when that faith grows into a large plant!

REFLECTION

- Have you or anyone you know ever experienced a Matthew 17:20 situation? If so, describe it.

- According to Matthew 13:23 how do we grow that seed of faith?

- What is one way you can start planting God's Word in your heart today to grow your faith?

FAITH FOCUS

Increase faith by

planting God's Word in your heart

"But he who received seed on the good ground
is he who hears the word and understands it,
who indeed bears fruit and produces:
some a hundredfold, some sixty, some thirty,"

Matthew 13: 23

PRAYER

Heavenly Father, write this Scripture on my heart as I read it out loud and write it in my Faith Notebook.

Heavenly Father, help me to see evidence of this Scripture today.

Record what you see, hear, or experience today that shows evidence of this Scripture.

DAY FIFTEEN

"Faith comes by hearing and hearing by the word of God."

Romans 10:17

WHAT DO I SAY?

What do I say? Pacing the floor, you think about what to say. I can't do this! Yes, yes, I can. You steal yourself and look into the mirror. Out loud, you practice your speech. "Hi, Eileen. You're looking good today. Want to go to a movie on Saturday night?" Nooo! You shake your head, thinking how lame you sound. You try again. "Hi, Eileen. I heard there was a good movie playing Saturday night. Would you like to go with me?" Humm, that sounds better. You repeat your speech over and over again out loud until you feel confident enough to face Eileen.

Whether it is asking for a first date, a raise at work, or pubic speaking, somehow, it builds our confidence to practice what we will say out loud. But it is more than an assumption that it builds our confidence, it is a Biblical principle. Confidence is another word for faith. The dictionary defines faith as: "complete trust or confidence in someone or something.[12]" Hebrews 11:1 (NIV) says, *"Now faith is confidence in what we hope for and assurance about what we do not see."* So, how do we gain more confidence or faith? That answer is found in Romans 10:17, *"Faith comes by hearing and hearing by the word of God."* Hearing the Word of God builds our confidence – our faith. Although thinking the Word of God is important, the Scripture says it's hearing the Word that builds our faith that God will do what we do not yet see. Like practicing the words to ask for a first date, hearing your voice speak God's words builds our confidence or faith. Is there an area of your life where you need to build your faith? Find a verse that applies to that area of your life and develop your faith by saying the verse out loud whenever you are in doubt. You may also want to add a verse about God's love as a reminder that God's love for you is unconditional and He wants to help you because God loves you so much.

Whatever verses you use, remember our loving heavenly Father wants to give us good gifts, Matthew 7:11, and the desires He has

[12] Dictionary.com

put in our hearts, Psalm 37:4-5. No matter what we face, our God can do all things for nothing is impossible for Him, Luke 1:37. Let's build our faith by speaking God's Word back to Him, even when we have not yet seen it come to pass.

REFLECTION

- In Romans 10:17, how do we build our faith?

- Describe one area of your life where you are having difficulties.

- What verse can you find that applies to your situation that you can speak out loud to build your faith? Write out the verse and pray it as a promise of God to you. For example: 2 Timothy 1:7 would be prayed, Thank you God that you have not given me a spirit of fear, but have given me a spirit of your power and of love and of a sound mind. I have faith that you will help me overcome (fill in your difficulty.)

FAITH FOCUS

Increase faith by speaking God's
Scriptures out loud to Him

"Faith comes by hearing and hearing by the word of God,"
Romans 10:17

PRAYER

Heavenly Father, write this Scripture on my heart as I read it out loud and write it in my Faith Notebook.

Heavenly Father, help me to see evidence of this Scripture today.

Record what you see, hear, or experience today that shows evidence of this Scripture.

"*Now this is the confidence that we have in Him, that if we ask anything according to His will, He hears us. And if we know that He hears us, whatever we ask, we know that we have the petitions that we have asked of Him.*"

1 John 5:14-15

WANT A COOKIE?

Do you remember as a child asking to have a cookie right before dinner? If you were in my house growing up, you would have heard my mom say, "Not now, it will spoil your appetite." So, what's a kid to do? Well, some of us grudgingly accepted our mom's decision, but others waited until she wasn't looking and would sneak a cookie, maybe even two, so they could hide one in their room for the next day. We didn't stop to reason that mom knew what was best for us or that if we got a cookie, our siblings would want one too. Even today, if I bake chocolate chip cookies close to dinner, I hear in my mind, "Not now, it will spoil your appetite." However, I love chocolate, so I indulge even knowing it is not in my best interest. Fess up, whether it is sneaking a cookie or indulging in something else, don't we all occasionally do things that are not in our best interest?

"Now this is the confidence that we have in Him, that if we ask anything according to His will, He hears us. And if we know that He hears us, whatever we ask, we know that we have the petitions that we have asked of Him," 1 John 5:14-15.

Does that mean we get anything we ask for even if it is a cookie before dinner? No, we need to pray according to God's will. Why? Because God in His great love for us wants to do what is in our best interest, even when we don't. He sees the bigger picture knowing not only what is best for us, but what is best for the others who would be impacted by our request. Just like mom recognized that it was in our best interest as well as our siblings to have an appetite for the right foods at dinner rather than a cookie.

When we know something is God's will, we can have the faith that God will answer our petitions. How do we know something is God's will?

1. **It follows God's Word.** God's will does not go against Scripture. *"God is not a man, that He should lie, nor a son of man,*

that He should repent. Has He said, and will He not do? Or has He spoken, and will He not make it good?" Numbers 23:19.

2. **It follows God's character.** *". . . God is love,"* 1 John 4:16. God's character is loving and exemplifies all the fruits of the Spirit; love, joy, peace, long-suffering, gentleness, goodness, faith, meekness, and moderation, Galatians 5:22-23.

3. **It glorifies God.** *"For all the promises of God in Him are Yes, and in Him Amen, to the glory of God through us,"* 2 Corinthians 1:20.

4. **Once you act on God's will, it brings peace, not confusion or torment.** *"But the wisdom that is from above is first pure, then peaceable, gentle, willing to yield, full of mercy and good fruits, without partiality and without hypocrisy,"* James 3:17.

Are you still unsure if something is God's will? The Lord directs us in Proverbs to seek counsel, *"A wise man will hear and increase learning, and a man of understanding will attain wise counsel,"* Proverbs 1:5. When unsure, I encourage you to find someone who has a heart for God that you trust hears from the Lord and pray together to hear the Lord's will. God loves us and wants us to know His will for us, which will always be in our best interest.

REFLECTION

- In your own words, summarize 1 John 5:14-15.

- Have you ever prayed for something that didn't happen? Looking back did it align with the criteria above?

- Describe something that you are presently praying for and evaluate whether it is God's will.

- Identify something that you know is God's will for you. Personalize 1 John 5:14-15 and include what you have identified as God's will. Pray what you write.

FAITH FOCUS

Increase faith by making sure
your request is God's will

"Now this is the confidence that we have in Him,
that if we ask anything according to His will,
He hears us. And if we know that He hears us,
whatever we ask, we know that we have the
petitions that we have asked of Him."

1 John 5:14-15

PRAYER

Heavenly Father, write this Scripture on
my heart as I read it out loud and write it
in my Faith Notebook.

Heavenly Father, help me to see
evidence of this Scripture today.

Record what you see, hear, or experience today
that shows evidence of this Scripture.

DAY SEVENTEEN

"Truly I tell you, if you have faith as small as a mustard seed, you can say to this mountain, 'Move from here to there,' and it will move. Nothing will be impossible for you."

Matthew 17:20

HOW MUCH?

Every day we have faith. Faith, we don't even recognize as, well, faith. When we apply our foot to the brakes of our car, we have faith that it will stop. We go home and have faith that our key will open the front door. We don't necessarily understand or even see the intricacies of how these things work, but we still have faith they will work. We often wonder if we have enough faith. We assume we need a considerable amount to be healed or receive answers to our prayers. But do we?

Faith — How much do we need?

"Truly I tell you, if you have faith as small as a mustard seed, you can say to this mountain, 'Move from here to there,' and it will move. Nothing will be impossible for you," Matthew 17:20.

In this verse, the word "faith" in the Strongs Greek #4102 means, "reliance upon Jesus for salvation." If we believe in Jesus, don't we all already have enough faith? If you have ever seen mustard seeds, they are approximately 1/16th of an inch in diameter. Not very big, are they? So basically, this verse is saying, if you have that little bitty 1/16" mustard seed size reliance upon Jesus for your salvation, nothing will be impossible for you.

In God's love for you, He already gave you all you needed when you believed in Him for your salvation – just a little bit of faith.

REFLECTION

- Rewrite Matthew 17:20 in your own words incorporating the definition of faith.

- Describe a challenge you currently face. According to Matthew 17:20, do you believe God has given you enough faith to overcome that challenge?

- How can you apply your faith to that challenge today? (hint, see Day 15)

FAITH FOCUS

Walk in faith, remembering all it takes is a little bit of faith to see the impossible in our lives

"Truly I tell you, if you have faith as small as a mustard seed, you can say to this mountain, 'Move from here to there,' and it will move. Nothing will be impossible for you,"

Matthew 17:20

PRAYER

Heavenly Father, write this Scripture on my heart as I read it out loud and write it in my Faith Notebook.

Heavenly Father, help me to see evidence of this Scripture today.

Record what you see, hear, or experience today that shows evidence of this Scripture.

Daily Scripture Reading
Allows You To
Grow Your Faith
One Day at a Time

DAY EIGHTEEN

"Ask, and it will be given to you, seek, and you will find, knock, and it will be opened to you."

Matthew 7:7

DO YOU FEEL IT?

Have you ever gone shopping and bought something you did not plan on buying? Honestly, who can say they haven't done that? My unplanned purchases usually are based on looks, not function. It was just so pretty! I loved the color! Then on the opposite end of the spectrum, some people purchase things for their features like gadgets, technology, etc. But the bottom line is that these impulse purchases are often made based on our emotions. The item just struck a chord with us, and so we bought it.

Well, we are all normal. Our emotions affect our decisions about most everything we do. What to buy, where to shop, where to live, our careers, etc. But how about our faith? Although our emotions impact our faith, God asks us to put them aside and trust in Him. Faith is not an emotion; it is a decision. People healed by Jesus made the decision to come to Him anticipating healing, Luke 6:17-19. Their decision was an act of faith.

It is easy to pray for a few days, not see a result and give up. But persistence pays off. I have a friend who persistently prayed 20 years for reconciliation with her daughter before she saw results. *"Ask, and it will be given to you, seek, and you will find, knock, and it will be opened to you,"* Matthew 7:7. The word "ask" in Strong's Greek #154 "denotes insistent asking without qualms, not "commanding" God, but solidly presenting a requisition whose items He longs to distribute.[13]"

If you have not yet seen a full manifestation of healing or answer to prayer, don't give up. Keep asking. Make the decision that no matter what your emotions are telling you that you will act in faith. God loves us so much that He wants to answer our prayer. Be persistent, don't give up and look to see what the God of the impossible will do! Mark 10:27, *But Jesus looked at them and said, "With men it is impossible, but not with God; for with God all things are possible."*

[13] Spirit Filled Life Bible, Word Wealth

REFLECTION

- Have you given up on asking God to answer a particular request?

- Describe the request. Does the request line up with God's will for you? (hint, see Day 16)

- What does Matthew 7:7 say about our persistence?

- What can you identify as God's will for you that you can start persistently praying for in faith today? Write a Scripture promise to help you personalize your prayer.

FAITH FOCUS

Walk in faith by making a decision
to act in faith persistently

"Ask, and it will be given to you,
seek, and you will find,
knock, and it will be opened to you,"
Matthew 7:7

PRAYER

Heavenly Father, write this Scripture on my heart as I read it out loud and write it in my Faith Notebook.

Heavenly Father, help me to see evidence of this Scripture today.

Record what you see, hear, or experience today
that shows evidence of this Scripture.

Daily Scripture Reading
Allows You To
Grow Your Faith
One Day at a Time

DAY NINETEEN

"But let him ask in faith, with no doubting, for he who doubts is like a wave of the sea driven and tossed by the wind. For let not that man suppose that he will receive anything from the Lord, he is a double-minded man, unstable in all his ways."

James 1:6-8

REVOLVING DOORS!

R ound, and around and around you go, where you stop, nobody knows! Looking for the revolving door to slow down, you jump in and push as you go around and around, bypassing the exit to your desired destination. Then you slow down and jump out. But do you stay out? Of course not! You continue to jump back in and back out, hoping to avoid getting whacked by the door! That is until you hear your father yelling, "Hurry up and get out of the revolving door!"

We often get stuck in a revolving door and don't even realize it. When we pray, then speak or act in opposition to our prayer, it is like getting stuck in a revolving door, where we keep missing our desired destination. When in faith, we ask the Lord to provide for us, we enter the door that will bring us to victory. However, we miss our desired destination when we act or speak contrary to our prayer of faith. Like with our finances. Have you ever prayed for the Lord to provide and then said things like, "I don't have enough to pay my bills" or "I can't afford that!" If we do that often enough, at some point, we are going to get whacked by the door as we exit out the wrong side with unanswered prayers. So why weren't our prayers answered?

"But let him ask in faith, with no doubting, for he who doubts is like a wave of the sea driven and tossed by the wind. For let not that man suppose that he will receive anything from the Lord; he is a double-minded man, unstable in all his ways," James 1:6-8. Speaking or acting in opposition to our prayers is being double-minded, and as this Scripture says, we will not receive anything from the Lord.

We don't need to deny reality, but we do want to avoid getting whacked by the revolving door by speaking or acting in faith as we trust our loving God to be victorious. So, what do we say when we are broke, and someone asks if we have enough money to pay our bills? Perhaps we say, "Not at this moment, but I trust the Lord will provide."

REFLECTION

- What does it mean to be double minded regarding our prayers?
- What does James 1:6-8 say about being double minded?
- Is there something you have been praying for that you believe is God's will but haven't received?
- Ask God to show you if you have spoken or acted in opposition to your prayer. Describe how you may have done this.
- Write how you can speak or act in faith.

FAITH FOCUS

Walk in faith by acting and speaking
in single-minded faith

"But let him ask in faith, with no doubting,
for he who doubts is like a wave of the sea
driven and tossed by the wind. For let not that man
suppose that he will receive anything from the Lord;
he is a double-minded man, unstable in all his ways,"
James 1:6-8

PRAYER

Heavenly Father, write this Scripture on my heart as I read it out loud and write it in my Faith Notebook.

Heavenly Father, help me to see evidence of this Scripture today.

Record what you see, hear, or experience today
that shows evidence of this Scripture.

Daily Scripture Reading
Allows You To
Grow Your Faith
One Day at a Time

DAY TWENTY

"All Scripture is given by inspiration of God and is profitable for doctrine, for reproof, for correction, for instruction in righteousness, that the man of God may be complete, thoroughly equipped for every good work."

2 Timothy 3:16-17

GOT QUESTIONS???

Have you ever had ants in your kitchen? We did, and it drove me nuts!! I searched every nook and cranny to see where they were entering. I did research on the Internet, looked at products in the store, read every label to make sure it was not dangerous for us or the dog, asked knowledgeable friends questions and even bought a book. I was not satisfied until I could get rid of every little black ant. Temporarily it was my passion.

When we have a problem that hounds us, we often make it our passion to find the solution, just like the ants and me. In the Scriptures, crowds would follow Jesus. Why? Because like all human beings, they had a problem. It could be emotional, physical, or spiritual. It didn't matter what it was. They sought Him for a solution. So, what did Jesus do? He taught. He could have waved His hand or spoken a few words to solve all of their problems. But He didn't – instead, He taught. Why? Maybe it is because if we are taught a solution, we know how to resolve the problem the next time we encounter it. Isn't that in our best interest? God loves us so much that He will do what will be in our best interest. Do you have a problem you need to have solved? Go to the greatest answer book of all time, the Bible, and let the Holy Spirit give you revelation. *"But the Helper, the Holy Spirit, whom the Father will send in My name, He will teach you all things, and bring to your remembrance all things that I said to you,"* John 14:26.

Just like I researched ants when I needed to get rid of them, investigate your specific problem with passion. Is it anxiety? Study every Scripture on anxiety and fear. How about finances? Study poverty and money. In addition to studying the problem, also explore the opposite topic. For example, in place of anxiety, we want peace, so also research peace. To study poverty, add the study of provision. For healing study Scriptures on sickness, healing, and health. God's Word will give us the answers we need, and we will be encouraged that God will solve our problem.

REFLECTION

- Rewrite John 14:26 and personalize it.

- Describe a problem that you can research today.

- Pray John 14:26 asking God to guide you to identify two Scriptures that address your problem. For example, for anxiety/stress Philippians 4:6,7

- Identify two Scriptures that are the opposite of your problem. For example; if the problem is anxiety/stress, research peace, Isaiah 26:3.

- How can you apply those Scriptures in faith as solutions to your problem? (hint Day 15, 18, 19)

FAITH FOCUS

Increase faith by researching God's Word
for solutions to your problems

*"All Scripture is given by inspiration of God
and is profitable for doctrine, for reproof,
for correction, for instruction in righteousness,
that the man of God may be complete,
thoroughly equipped for every good work,"*
2 Timothy 3:16-17

PRAYER

Heavenly Father, write this Scripture on my heart as I read it out loud and write it in my Faith Notebook.

Heavenly Father, help me to see evidence of this Scripture today.

Record what you see, hear, or experience today that shows evidence of this Scripture.

DAY TWENTY-ONE

"Therefore I say to you, whatever things you ask when you pray, believe that you receive them, and you will have them."

Mark 11:24

KEEP ON GOING!

Just imagine exploring a beautiful cave. You are surrounded by towering stone formations, water dripping down icicle shaped stalactites into mirrored pools and stalagmites rising from the cave floor like an icicle garden. The deeper you go, the colder, darker, and damper it becomes. BOOM! The noise explodes in your ears as rocks pour down around you pitching you into complete darkness. Possibly hurt and surrounded by rubble you realize that there is no apparent way out! Ahh!

We hear stories about people with just such experiences. How do they escape their situation and survive? From what I have read, it seems to be by sheer persistence, determination, and probably prayer. In situations like that, the choice is to either cower in fear and accept that there is no hope or decide to fight for survival. Those who make it must persistently focus on the goal of survival with hope, courage, and determination as they look for ways to escape. No matter what they encounter, they keep going.

We may never, I pray, be trapped in a cave, but we may be in a situation that requires persistently focusing on the goal to survive. Jairus faced such a situation as his daughter's survival depended on his persistence and hope in Jesus. In Luke 8:40-42, 49-55, Jairus' daughter was sick and dying. Jarius went to Jesus to ask Him to come and heal her. Why? He must have trusted not only in Jesus' power to heal but in His loving character. He must have known that Jesus would care enough to help his daughter. As Jesus and Jairus traveled to his home, they received word that his daughter was dead, but Jesus said, *"Do not be afraid, only believe, and she will be made well,"* Luke 8:50.

At this point, Jairus could have given up, but he chose to push aside the fear and to trust and hope in Jesus. Jesus could have healed her at that moment, but apparently, it wasn't God's perfect timing yet. Upon reaching his home, they met those mourning his daughter's death. Once again, Jairus could have given up and joined the doubters who ridiculed Jesus when Jesus said, *"Do not weep; she is not dead, but sleeping,"* Luke 8:52. But he didn't. No matter what the circumstances, Jairus kept his eyes on Jesus, trusting in Him. Jairus pushed aside his fears, refused to dwell on the negative no matter what, persistently moved forward, and received the answer to his request – his daughter was brought back to life!

When faced with challenges like Jairus or someone trapped in a cave, trusting in God's loving heart for us, even when we can't immediately see answers, allows us to persistently pray and move forward in the faith that our prayers will be answered in God's perfect timing. Trusting God's character of love, faithfulness to us, and His promises is a key to answered prayer. But how do we trust amid challenges?

1. **Keep our mind focused on Jesus.** *"You will keep him in perfect peace, Whose mind is stayed on You, Because he trusts in You,"* Isaiah 26:3.

2. **Refuse to dwell on negative thoughts and our fears. Instead, meditate on Scripture that emphasizes God's loving character and promises.** *"But God, who is rich in mercy, because of His great love with which He loved us,"* Ephesians 2:4.

3. **Ask God for strength to keep persistently moving forward and to help us if we fall into doubt.** *"I can do all things through Christ who strengthens me,"* Philippians 4:13.

4. **Be persistent by continuing to ask.** *"Ask, and it will be given to you; seek, and you will find; knock, and it will be opened to you. For everyone who asks receives, and he who seeks finds, and to him who knocks it will be opened,"* Matthew 7:7-8.

With courage, persistent faith, and focus, we will see answered prayers in His perfect timing in His perfect way.

REFLECTION

- Describe a difficult situation you are facing.

- Are there any negative thoughts you may be dwelling on about your situation? For example: "This will never change." "Things are only getting worse."

- Rewrite Mark 11:24 personalizing it.

- Identify at least one Scripture you can focus on in faith to combat those negative, unbelieving thoughts.

FAITH FOCUS

Walk in faith by being persistent
and not giving up!

*"Therefore I say to you, whatever things you ask
when you pray, believe that you receive them,
and you will have them,"*

Mark 11:24

PRAYER

Heavenly Father, write this Scripture on my heart as I read it out loud and write it in my Faith Notebook.

Heavenly Father, help me to see evidence of this Scripture today.

Record what you see, hear, or experience today
that shows evidence of this Scripture.

ENRICHMENT STEP 3
Day 14-21

I. This week let's literally plant a seed to parallel planting God's Word in our hearts as in Day 14. Whether it's the seed of God's Word or a plant, in both cases to grow them we need; research, good ground, water and light. There are two parts to this exercise; literally planting a seed and planting God's Word.

Part 1 – Planting a literal seed. (You need; a pot, seed and soil.)

- Identify the type of seed you want to plant.

- Research the type of soil it needs, amount of water and type of light required.

- Provide good ground by acquiring the type of soil needed, soften the soil by breaking it up as you place it in the pot further insuring it is planted in good ground.

- Plant your seed.

- Water your seed as directed by your research.

- Place the pot where it will receive proper light.

Part 2 – Planting God's Word. (You will need a Bible, pen and a sheet of paper.)

- Identify an issue where you are struggling to believe in faith that God will be victorious.

- Research God's Word to find Scriptures to plant addressing your issue just like you researched the needs for planting your seed. Select at least three Scriptures as directed below to plant, water and light your way.

- Good ground to receive God's Word has already been made in your heart when you decided to do this enrichment activity. It shows your desire to grow your faith and relationship with God who wants to grow His relationship of love with you.

- Plant. Write on your paper a Scripture you want to plant in your heart to increase your faith that either generally addresses faith (example Matthew 17:20) or directly addresses your challenging issue.

- Water. Write a Scripture you want to plant in your heart to increase your faith that directly addresses your challenging issue.

- Light. Write a Scripture you can pray asking our loving God to light your understanding to increase your faith. (For example; Isaiah. 58:8, Galatians 1:12, Ephesians 1:17)

- Post the list by the seed you planted. Each time you water the seed in the pot, read and pray the Scriptures out loud to grow your faith.

Now, believe that your seeds of faith will grow as you nurture your relationship with God just like that little bitty seed you planted in the pot will grow as you nurture it too.

2. The last question in the Reflection section of Days 14-21, tells you an action to take such as praying persistently, speaking in faith, etc. Select one of those actions that you feel would most benefit you and make that a part of your daily routine.

DAY TWENTY-TWO

"Trust in the LORD with all your heart, and lean not on your own understanding, In all your ways acknowledge Him, And He shall direct your paths."

Proverbs 3:5-6

ONE STEP AT A TIME!

"I have to cross that?!" you exclaim. With wide eyes, you look out over this incredibly deep, vast canyon and see this little bitty swinging bridge made of rope. Now, what was the person thinking that made a bridge out of rope? They sure were not thinking of the people who needed to cross it! We, who look out over the canyon in fear, need to build up some chutzpah to walk even one step. Taking a deep breath and looking straight ahead, we take the first step. Each step is a challenge. We hold on so tightly that our knuckles turn white, praying that God will keep us safe as we carefully take each step while avoiding looking at the canyon below. We can't think about all the steps that are left to conquer, we can only think about the next one on our path. Then after what seems like an hour but was only an agonizing few minutes, we suddenly discover that we have safely made it to the other side! Yeah! So how do you cross a swinging bridge? One step at a time!

When we think about it, we tackle many things, one small piece at a time. How do you eat a big meal? One bite at a time! How do you drive to Florida? One mile at a time! But sometimes we look at a problem and just get overwhelmed. So, when we are faced with overwhelming challenges, how can we get through them? Just like the swinging bridge, a meal, or a trip, we can get through a problem one step at a time. God said, don't worry about what is ahead, *"Therefore do not worry about tomorrow, for tomorrow will worry about its' own things. Sufficient for the day is its' own trouble,"* Matthew 6:34.

God does not intend for us to be overwhelmed by the enormity of a situation, but to pray and trust in Him to guide us through step by step by step. Take one small piece of the problem at a time, release it to God in prayer, and trust that He will guide you to resolve the situation. *"Trust in the LORD with all your heart, and lean not on your own understanding; In all your ways acknowledge Him, And He shall direct your paths,"* Proverbs 3:5-6.

When we look to God and pray, our loving God will give us whatever we need at the moment we need it and guide us through so that we can be victorious. Then one day, we will look back and see we have made it safely and victoriously to the other side of our problem as He promised. *"Yet in all these things we are more than conquerors through Him who loved us,"* Romans 8:37.

REFLECTION

- What promise does God make to us in Proverbs 3:5-6?
- Describe one issue you currently face.
- Ask God how you can break that issue into smaller pieces and write out your plan.
- What small piece can you have faith to believe God for today?

FAITH FOCUS

Increase faith by seeing success in tackling problems one small step at a time

*"Trust in the LORD with all your heart,
and lean not on your own understanding;
In all your ways acknowledge Him,
And He shall direct your paths,"*

Proverbs 3:5-6

PRAYER

Heavenly Father, write this Scripture on my heart as I read it out loud and write it in my Faith Notebook.

Heavenly Father, help me to see evidence of this Scripture today.

Record what you see, hear, or experience today that shows evidence of this Scripture.

DAY TWENTY-THREE

*"Casting all your
care upon Him,
for He cares for you."*

1 Peter 5:7

GET OUT OF THE DIRT!

Standing before the big pile of dirt, Jill and John turn to each other with smiles as they both shout, "MUD PIES!" Running to get a bucket of water, they return and pour it onto the dirt. Giggling, they let the mud ooze between their fingers as they form the creation they imagined, mud pies! What do they do with the excess mud on their hands? Why they wipe the excess mud on their shorts and shirts, of course! Been there and done that? If not, you may have children or grandchildren who did. What happened when the pies were finished? An adult brings out the garden hose to hose them down! No way, was a mud slathered child bringing that mess into the clean house!

So, what do mud pies and problems have in common? They both stick to you and make a mess! How do we prevent that? By staying out of the dirt! Problems are like dirt. They soil our clean and joyful thoughts. When we have a problem, we have a tendency to focus on it, letting our imagination create a mess. Talking and thinking about the "dirt" just gives us a bigger pile of dirt.

We can't avoid all problems, but there is a way to prevent it from soiling our thoughts and sticking to us. The Scripture says, *"Casting all your care upon Him, for He cares for you,"* 1 Peter 5:7. No matter how big or small the problem, He wants them all because He loves us. Praying and giving our problems to God is the first step to get rid of the "dirt." To get "clean," we need to change our focus. If we focus on God and the Scriptures and His ability to resolve the problem, He will help us not to create a mess for ourselves. His Scripture is like a garden hose that soaks us with His Word and cleanses our thoughts. *"That He might sanctify and cleanse her with the washing of water by the word,"* Ephesians 5:26. Let's all turn our problems over to God and allow ourselves to be soaked in His Word.

REFLECTION

- Is there a problem that has stuck to you like mud, soiled your thoughts or created a mess in your mind as you imagine all the "what if" negative results? Describe that problem.

- How can you apply Ephesians 5:26 to get rid of muddy thoughts?

- In your own words rewrite and personalize 1 Peter 5:7 substituting your problem for the word "cares." Pray what you have written and give your problem to God.

- What Scripture can you find that helps you to focus your thoughts in faith? Pray that Scripture whenever muddy thoughts come.

FAITH FOCUS

Walk in faith by focusing on God
and not the problem.

"Casting all your care upon Him, for He cares for you,"

1 Peter 5:7

PRAYER

Heavenly Father, write this Scripture on my heart as I read it out loud and write it in my Faith Notebook.

Heavenly Father, help me to see evidence of this Scripture today.

Record what you see, hear, or experience today
that shows evidence of this Scripture.

Daily Scripture Reading
Allows You To
Grow Your Faith
One Day at a Time

DAY TWENTY-FOUR

"To everything there is a season, A time for every purpose under heaven: "

Ecclesiastes 3:1

Ch-ch-ch-ch-CHANGES!

Ahhh! No power! Although we have come to expect our typical summer season to be hot and dry one day and the next, humid and stormy, I am always surprised by the intense storms that bring flooding, downed trees, and the dreaded – LOSS OF POWER! Geez, when you lose power, everything changes. First of all, it is H-O-T, HOT! Then, you have to read by a flashlight because TV is not an option. And of course, food! You either venture out to eat almost every meal, or you survive on peanut butter and jelly. I don't know about you, but I can only eat so much peanut butter and jelly. Fortunately, during the last storm, it was not too unpleasant because we stayed with my mother, who had air conditioning and a refrigerator, yay! Even so, with the subsequent storms we have had, I find myself thinking like our friends' granddaughter, who said, "OH NO! Are we going to lose power again!" Then I have to remind myself that God is in charge and to be thankful that these storms are only for a season.

"To everything there is a season, A time for every purpose under heaven: A time to be born, And a time to die; A time to plant, And a time to pluck what is planted; A time to kill, And a time to heal; A time to break down, And a time to build up; A time to weep, And a time to laugh; A time to mourn, And a time to dance; A time to cast away stones, And a time to gather stones; A time to embrace, And a time to refrain from embracing; A time to gain, And a time to lose; A time to keep, And a time to throw away; A time to tear, And a time to sew; A time to keep silence, And a time to speak; A time to love, And a time to hate, A time of war, And a time of peace," Ecclesiastes 3:1-8.

The Scriptures tell us that there is a season for everything. Change, even when it is unexpected or unpleasant like the storm, is part of life. How we view it will impact how we get through it. If, like me, your first reaction is to fearfully anticipate the worst with each new storm, you will be miserable until you turn it over to God. We have a choice if we react in fear, to either stay in fear or to turn to God and trust God to take care of us. When we give it to God, He promises to provide us with something in return - peace. *"Be anxious for nothing, but in everything by prayer and supplication, with thanksgiving, let your requests be made known to God; and the peace of God, which surpasses all understanding, will guard your hearts and minds through Christ Jesus,"* Philippians 4: 6-7.

For everything, there is a season. When you are in the midst of changes in your life, remember it is only for a season. God loves us and wants to help us through all seasons. Let's be thankful and pray, giving even the unpleasant, unexpected changes to God. He ultimately is the only one who can give us back the gift of peace. Sim Shalom (grant peace).

REFLECTION

- What changes are you going through?
- Select the season(s) that currently apply to you in Ecclesiastes 3:1-8. What perspective do these verses give you?
- What four things does Philippians 4:6-7 direct us to do about anxiety and what will be the result of following God's directions?
- How can you apply the above verses in Ecclesiastes and Philippians to walk in faith through the changes you are experiencing?

FAITH FOCUS

Walk in faith by remembering that the

storms of life are only for a season.

"To everything there is a season,
A time for every purpose under heaven: "

Ecclesiastes 3:1

PRAYER

Heavenly Father, write this Scripture on my heart as I read it out loud and write it in my Faith Notebook.

Heavenly Father, help me to see evidence of this Scripture today.

Record what you see, hear, or experience today that shows evidence of this Scripture.

DAY TWENTY-FIVE

"This Book of the Law shall not depart from your mouth, but you shall meditate in it day and night, that you may observe to do according to all that is written in it. For then you will make your way prosperous, and then you will have good success. Have I not commanded you? Be strong and of good courage, do not be afraid, nor be dismayed, for the LORD your God is with you wherever you go."

Joshua 1:8-9

WE WANT RESULTS NOW!

We plant bulbs in the fall, but we don't see them until the spring. Many of us will have the faith that the wait is just the process of nature and that we will see flowers in the spring. Then there are those like me who are unskilled gardeners. Because we don't see them and don't have faith in our skills, we may wonder if the flowers will really come up. We need to see the results of our work now.

Doesn't our faith in God feel like that sometimes? We take that teeny tiny mustard seed of faith and implant it in our heart, and then we wait for results. Sometimes we wait and wait and wait some more. Occasionally, we may have faith that the Lord is working through the waiting even though we don't see results. Other times, we may wonder if we will ever really get an answer. We want instant gratification, but God wants us to exercise our faith.

No muscle will develop and gain strength unless we exercise it. It may take muscles to dig that hole to plant our tiny seeds, but what muscles does the gardener exercise when they are waiting from fall till spring? The muscle of faith.

Just like the gardener believes by faith that those bulbs will be flowers, we can exercise our faith by believing and meditating on His Word knowing that the Lord promises results, *"This Book of the Law shall not depart from your mouth, but you shall meditate in it day and night, that you may observe to do according to all that is written in it. For then you will make your way prosperous, and then you will have good success,"* Joshua 1:8.

Let's all exercise our faith in those times of waiting. And when we are waiting for our answers, remember Joshua 1:9 *"Have I not commanded you? Be strong and of good courage; do not be afraid, nor be dismayed, for the LORD your God is with you wherever you go."* The Lord has not left us. He loves us, and He is with us even when we don't see answers yet.

REFLECTION

- What do you need faith for today?
- What action does Joshua 1:8 tell us to do that will exercise your faith muscles?
- What Scripture promise can you meditate on to help you exercise faith for what you need today?

FAITH FOCUS

Increase your faith by exercising
your faith muscles by
believing and meditating on God's Word

"This Book of the Law shall not depart from your mouth,
but you shall meditate in it day and night, that you
may observe to do according to all that is written in it.
For then you will make your way prosperous,
and then you will have good success.
Have I not commanded you?
Be strong and of good courage;
do not be afraid, nor be dismayed,
for the LORD your God
is with you wherever you go,"

Joshua 1:8-9

PRAYER

Heavenly Father, write this Scripture on my heart as I read it out loud and write it in my Faith Notebook.

Heavenly Father, help me to see evidence of this Scripture today.

Record what you see, hear, or experience today that shows evidence of this Scripture.

DAY TWENTY-SIX

"*For God has not given us a spirit of fear, but of power and of love and of a sound mind.*"

2 Timothy 1:7

IT'S WORTH THE FIGHT!

Did you ever play sports growing up? If so, you may recall that with sports, there is usually a learning curve that involves falling down, getting hit by a ball or a person, and having lots of bruises. How agile you were or how quickly you learned, determined how many injuries you got before you learned the skills required for the game.

We probably all remember those days when we had to play baseball in PE class. When the ball was thrown, some classmates ran towards it with relish, others moved out of the way, and still, others just stood there and let it hit them. Depending upon our experience, the next baseball game in PE was faced with either joy, dread, or outright fear as we thought about and dwelled upon our previous experience. Some classmates with bad experiences gave into fear magnifying the event to the extent that they developed sudden injuries or illnesses, real or faked, to avoid playing. Others may have fought their fears facing them with determination to overcome them even at the risk of repeating a bad experience. They moved forward in faith, focusing on having a better experience.

When bad things happen, it is not unusual to experience fear. We anticipate the experience will happen to us again or even to someone we love. Just like in PE class, we had a choice in how we would face the next baseball game, we also have a choice in how we face the painful or bad experiences in life. But the Lord does not want us to face them in fear or to face them alone.

Fear is more than a reaction; it can be a consuming and even immobilizing thought. When we react in fear and dwell on those thoughts which anticipate adverse outcomes, the fear only grows. But God has given us the power to overcome, a sound mind to recognize fearful thoughts and His love to provide us with peace,

"For God has not given us a spirit of fear, but of power and of love and of a sound mind," 2 Timothy 1:7. Whether it is disease, rejection, finances, or provision, it is not always easy to push fearful thoughts aside. But by using the tools God gave us, we can combat fear:

- **God gave us power,** *"Yet in all these things we are more than conquerors through Him who loved us,"* Romans 8:37.

- **God gave us His love,** *"There is no fear in love; but perfect love casts out fear, because fear involves torment . . ."* 1 John 4:18.

- **God gave us a sound mind,** *"You will keep him in perfect peace, whose mind is stayed on You, because he trusts in You,"* Isaiah 26:3.

These tools will help us to push those fearful thoughts aside as we focus our thoughts on God, remember how much He loves us and stand strong in His power. With God, we can be victorious over our fears.

REFLECTION

- Is there a situation which causes you to react in fear, real or perceived? Describe it.

- Is that a fear you want to destroy?

- In 2 Timothy 1:7, what tools has God given us to overcome fear and how can we use those tools?

- How can you apply those tools to the situation you fear so that you walk in faith? Be specific.

FAITH FOCUS

Walk in faith by focusing our thoughts on God
and not fearing a bad experience

"For God has not given us a spirit of fear,
but of power and of love and of a sound mind,"
2 Timothy 1:7

PRAYER

Heavenly Father, write this Scripture on my heart as I read it out loud and write it in my Faith Notebook.

Heavenly Father, help me to see evidence of this Scripture today.

Record what you see, hear, or experience today that shows evidence of this Scripture.

DAY TWENTY-SEVEN

"Fear not, for I am with you, Be not dismayed, for I am your God. I will strengthen you, Yes, I will help you, I will uphold you with My righteous right hand."

Isaiah 41:10

AHHHHH!

The rain falls in torrents, sounds of crashing thunder reverberates through the air mixed with the howling of the wind as darkness descends. Debris flies around the couple racing through the storm to the shelter of the abandoned house. As they enter, the man blindly searches until he finds a light switch, but it doesn't work. They carefully walk through the house, moving with the flashes of lightning as they search for a place to hunker down for the night. You watch the scene unfold on the movie screen, sitting tensely in your chair. As the music crescendos, you anticipate something dreadful is about to happen. Your jaw clenches, your shoulders tighten, and your hands grip the chair as you wait to see what happens next. Suddenly lightning flashes on the movie screen, revealing a third person in the room, the room plunges into darkness, and you hear a scream, AHHHH! You jump in your seat, startled by the scream. Even though you know you are safe and are only watching a movie, your body reacts in fear.

What is fear?[14]

> F - false
> E - evidence
> A - appearing
> R - real

Fear, anxiety, and stress are all the same. Whether it is pressure at work, your health, or financial issues, we all feel it at some time or another. We anticipate the worse, and it plays over and over in our minds until we are convinced that our worse fears are not false but are a reality. This false fear denies that God can be victorious over anything we encounter. It makes our bodies tense and can eventually affect our health if we remain in a state of tension for long periods.

[14] Be in Health

The Scriptures encourage us to "fear not" or "do not be afraid" over 59 times. God does not ask us to deny reality but to trust Him that He can give us a victorious outcome no matter what evidence we see to the contrary. God did not give us fear.

Whenever you feel fear, anxiety or stress remember:

- **God gave you power, love, and a sound mind to combat the enemy,** *"For God has not given us a spirit of fear, but of power and of love and of a sound mind,"* 2 Timothy 1:7.

- **That God is with you,** *"And the LORD, He is the One who goes before you. He will be with you, He will not leave you nor forsake you; do not fear nor be dismayed,"* Deuteronomy 31:8.

- **God can give you peace,** *"Peace I leave with you, My peace I give to you; not as the world gives do I give to you. Let not your heart be troubled, neither let it be afraid,"* John 14:27.

- **God can be victorious even in the face of earthly reality,** *"Behold, I am the LORD, the God of all flesh. Is there anything too hard for Me?"* Jeremiah 32:27.

REFLECTION

- Identify a situation that caused you fear, anxiety or stress.

- What truths in Deuteronomy 31:8, 2 Timothy 1:7 and John 14:27 can you hold onto when facing that situation?

- How does Jeremiah 32:27 apply to any situation causing you fear, anxiety or stress?

- Utilizing what you read today and on Day 26, what steps can you take to destroy your fear, anxiety or stress and replace it with faith?

FAITH FOCUS

Walk in faith, not denying reality

but trusting God to be victorious over it

"Fear not, for I am with you; Be not dismayed,
for I am your God. I will strengthen you,
Yes, I will help you, I will uphold you with
My righteous right hand,"

Isaiah 41:10

PRAYER

Heavenly Father, write this Scripture on my heart as I read it out loud and write it in my Faith Notebook.

Heavenly Father, help me to see evidence of this Scripture today.

Record what you see, hear, or experience today
that shows evidence of this Scripture.

DAY TWENTY-EIGHT

"*Remember His marvelous works which He has done, His wonders, and the judgments of His mouth.*"

1 Chronicles 16:12.

I REMEMBER!

Commercial jingles! Those jingles stick in your head, and just when you think they are forgotten, you see the product and BAM! The jingle is in your head again! Advertisers use commercial jingles, so we will remember the product. Let's try a few to see if you can remember and fill in the products. "My bologna has a first name; it's _ _ _ _ _." If you guessed O-S-C-A-R for Oscar Mayer, you are right. How about another old one from 1971 that was released as a pop song and replayed on several TV shows; "I'd like to teach the world to sing in perfect harmony." That, of course, is the famous Coke song. If you are too young for those, how about "You deserve a break today at _____." Why it's McDonald's, of course! This last one is for all ages since it was used in commercials for over 18 years, "Gimme a break, break me off a piece of that_____." It's a Kit Kat Bar![15] Are you hungry yet?

Like advertisers want us to remember their product, God wants us to remember the works that He has done, *"Remember His marvelous works which He has done, His wonders, and the judgments of His mouth,"* 1 Chronicles 16:12. God's works may not be in the form of a jingle, but God does use sights, sounds, smells, and people to bring things to our remembrance.

During the Jewish Passover Seder, they remember what God did. God brought the Israelites out of their bondage to the Egyptians into freedom. The Scriptures tell the Jews to remember, *"You shall eat no leavened bread with it; seven days you shall eat unleavened bread with it, that is, the bread of affliction (for you came out of the land of Egypt in haste), that you may remember the day in which you came out of the land of Egypt all the days of your life,"* Deuteronomy 16:3.

But why? Let me answer that with a question. Have you ever been anxious about the future? I think we all would respond yes to that question. So then how did you find peace? Perhaps by remembering something God did in the past to bring a solution?

[15] All commercial jingles from Wikipedia.com

Maybe that is one reason why God tells us to remember. In His infinite wisdom, He knows we humans all get anxious at one time or another. But when we stop and focus on remembering how God showed His power, mercy, and love in difficult situations in the past, it gives us confidence that what He has done before, He can do again, *"Jesus Christ is the same yesterday, today, and forever,"* Hebrews 13:8.

So, when we are faced with difficult situations, let's remember what God has done. Having trouble remembering? Then pray and ask God to remind you of all He has done. We may not always understand the way God works, but we can count on His love and mercy to do what is ultimately in our best interest even when it doesn't seem that way at first.

REFLECTION

- How does God encourage us in 1 Chronicles 16:12 and Hebrews 13:8?

- Does a particular sight, sound, smell or person bring to your memory something positive God or a person has done in your life? (Remember God uses people too.)

- How will remembering that event impact your perspective when a similar event occurs?

- What past event can you remember that will encourage your faith for something you are facing now?

FAITH FOCUS

Increase your faith by remembering
what God has done

"Remember His marvelous works which He has done,

His wonders, and the judgments of His mouth,"

1 Chronicles 16:12.

PRAYER

Heavenly Father, write this Scripture on my heart as I read it out loud and write it in my Faith Notebook.

Heavenly Father, help me to see evidence of this Scripture today.

Record what you see, hear, or experience today that shows evidence of this Scripture.

DAY TWENTY-NINE

"But as it is written: Eye has not seen, nor ear heard, Nor have entered into the heart of man The things which God has prepared for those who love Him. But God has revealed them to us through His Spirit. For the Spirit searches all things, yes, the deep things of God."

1 Corinthians 2:9-10

Watch That Ant!

Did you ever own an ant farm as a child? Or maybe sat in fascination as you watched the ants work on the mound in your yard? From our perspective, they look like little bitty insects that we could squash at any time. But, ants must have a different perspective, because they have survived as long as the earth.

Ants are such survivors and so determined that there has even been a song written about them, *High Hopes*;[16]

> Just what makes that little old ant
> Think he'll move that rubber tree plant
> Anyone knows an ant, can't
> Move a rubber tree plant
> But he's got high hopes, he's got high hopes
> He's got high apple pie, in the sky hopes
> So any time you're gettin' low
> 'Stead of lettin' go
> Just remember that ant
> Oops there goes another rubber tree plant.

Ants live in colonies, and "Ant societies have a division of labor, communication between individuals, and an ability to solve complex problems."[17] Hum, sounds kind of like us doesn't it? Of all creatures, a little bitty ant should look at problems and say, "I am too small. No way can I handle that!" But ants are clearly determined survivors. Their perseverance helps them as they face challenges, which could only be based on the perspective of what they can see, what they can hear, and what they know.

1 Corinthians 2:9-10 says, *"But as it is written: Eye has not seen, nor ear heard, nor have entered into the heart of man the things which God has prepared for those who love Him. But God has revealed them to us through His Spirit. For the Spirit searches all things, yes, the deep*

[16] James Van Heusen and Sammy Cahn
[17] Wikipedia

things of God." What is this verse saying? It is telling us that we, probably like the ants, gain our perspective on things by what we see and hear. Some of our perspectives come from our emotions. But God has a better way for us to face challenges – by seeing His perspective. God's perspective on things is revealed to us by His Holy Spirit.

Look at the example of Abraham. In Genesis 22, Abraham was asked by God to sacrifice his only son, Isaac, whom he loved. Can you imagine sacrificing someone you love? What torment Abraham must have endured. But, as you read the text, you do not get a picture of agony. In fact, it appears that Abraham acted so normal that his son had no idea what was to take place. When Isaac asked where the lamb was for the sacrifice, Abraham assured him that God would provide a lamb. I can only conclude that Abraham's perspective was not based on what his eyes could see or his ears could hear or what his emotions were yelling. Abraham must have had a revelation of the situation through the Holy Spirit. Abraham had to have had the perspective of God, and that was where he placed his hope.

So, let's all be as determined as the ant, but ask God to give us His perspective so that we put our high hopes and trust in Him. Knowing that God will provide answers or whatever is needed because He loves us so much.

REFLECTION

- What situation seems stressful or overwhelming to you? Why?
- Rewrite 1 Corinthians 2:9-10 in your own words, including how to identify God's perspective.
- Write what you feel is God's perspective on your situation.
- How can you apply God's perspective to help you walk in faith about your situation?

FAITH FOCUS

Walk in faith by asking God
to show us His perspective

*"But as it is written: Eye has not seen, nor ear heard, Nor
have entered into the heart of man The things which God
has prepared for those who love Him.
But God has revealed them to us through His Spirit.
For the Spirit searches all things, yes, the deep things of God,"*

1 Corinthians 2:9-10

PRAYER

Heavenly Father, write this Scripture on my heart as I read it out loud and write it in my Faith Notebook.

Heavenly Father, help me to see evidence of this Scripture today.

Record what you see, hear, or experience today
that shows evidence of this Scripture.

DAY THIRTY

"*And we know that all things work together for good to those who love God, to those who are the called according to His purpose.*"

Romans 8:28

BAD TO GOOD!

WHOOP, WHOOP, WHOOP! The blaring sound and flashing lights make you panic as the police car pulls up behind you. Oh, man, you think. What have I done, and how much will this cost me? Have you ever gotten a traffic ticket? Maybe you have never had this experience, but I have. I had no idea that I was going seven, yes, seven miles over the speed limit. At first, I was upset, but after a few days of stewing, I had to admit that I had gotten a little lax about my driving, which is never a very good thing. It screams – Potential Accident! Watch Out! So actually, in that regard, the ticket was a good thing. No, I am not just saying that – I really believe that it was a wake-up call to be a better driver.

Getting a ticket was terrible on my nerves and my pocketbook, but God promised He would work ALL things for good and He did by improving my driving, *"And we know that all things work together for good to those who love God, to those who are the called according to His purpose,"* Romans 8:28.

In the Scriptures, when we read the Book of Esther, we see examples of how God continually worked terrible things for good throughout the story. Here is how:

- **Bad** – Esther's parents died when she was young.
- **Good** – She was brought to live with a godly man, her relative Mordecai, in the province of King Ahasuerus. Living in the province would allow her to fulfill God's purpose for her life. (Esther 2:7)
- **Bad** – During a banquet, King Ahasuerus commanded Queen Vashti's appearance. She refused to come and was removed as queen. (Esther 1:12)
- **Good** – The opportunity arose for a new queen to be chosen. Esther was chosen as a candidate. She received favor in beauty preparations, and housing from the king who loved her and made her queen. (Esther 1:15-19, 2:8, 9,15,19)

- **Bad** – There was a plot to kill King Ahasuerus. (Esther 2:21)
- **Good** – Mordecai overheard the plot. He informed Esther who told the king in Mordecai's name. The plot was thwarted and recorded in the king's records. (Esther 2:22-23)
- **Bad** – Haman was promoted over the king's officials. He hated and planned to destroy all the Jews. (Esther 3:1,6, 8-13) To thwart Haman's plan, Esther needed to intervene with the king, but to approach him without being summoned could result in her death. (Esther 4:10-11)
- **Good** – Esther trusted the Lord and called for prayer and fasting. In faith, she approached the king and was received by him, so her life was spared. (Esther 4:16, 5:2)

Well, I could go on and on but you get the picture. Over and over again, the Lord turned bad things to good. The ultimate good of the story is that the king protected the Jews, destroyed Haman, honored Mordecai, and allowed the Jews' tormentors to be destroyed. (Esther Chapters 7-9)

Don't lose faith when bad things happen. Let's remember how the Lord can turn ALL things to good for those who love Him. It doesn't matter if it is a good thing or a bad thing because He promises to turn ALL things to good when we love Him because of His great love for us.

REFLECTION

- Rewrite and personalize Romans 8:28.
- List four ways God can use bad situations for good. (You may get some ideas from Esther above.)
- Identify a bad thing that has happened in your life. Looking back, how has God used it for good?
- How can Romans 8:28 help you walk in faith in a current bad situation?

FAITH FOCUS

Increase faith by reminding yourself
that God can use even bad things for good

*"And we know that all things work together for good
to those who love God, to those who are the called
according to His purpose,"*

Romans 8:28

PRAYER

Heavenly Father, write this Scripture on
my heart as I read it out loud and write it
in my Faith Notebook.

Heavenly Father, help me to see
evidence of this Scripture today.

Record what you see, hear, or experience today
that shows evidence of this Scripture.

My brethren, count it all joy when you fall into various trials, knowing that the testing of your faith produces patience."

James 1:2-3

SHAAKKEENN!

The floor shakes beneath your feet as your coffee sloshes out of your cup. You watch chairs dance around the room. Thud! Crash! Books fall, and objects shatter into hundreds of pieces as they scatter across the floor. Suddenly everything is still. The earthquake is over. Your eyes sweep the room, taking in the devastation and damage to the building. You close your eyes and take a deep breath to calm your nerves. "Now, what out of all this mess can I be thankful for? Oh well, I guess I can be thankful that the earthquake shaking has exposed weaknesses to the building's structure." Then you realize that this exposure will allow you to remove the weak building materials and replace them with stronger materials so that the building can stand stronger when the next earthquake comes.

You may not have experienced an earthquake, but all of us have been shaken at some time or another. Shaken with an unexpected death, shaken when trust is broken, shaken with the loss of a job, and shaken with any of the other major changes that most people talk about. But, there is one thing that most people don't talk about – when they have believed in faith for something that doesn't happen, they may be shaken in their faith.

We usually consider the experiences or trials that shake us as adverse events. But, we get a different perspective from James 1:2-4, *"My brethren, count it all joy when you fall into various trials, knowing that the testing of your faith produces patience. But let patience have its perfect work, that you may be perfect and complete, lacking nothing."* Joy! You have got to be kidding me, right?

Well, let's look at these "trials" like an earthquake. An earthquake tests the strength of a building like a trial tests the strength of our faith. Just like the weaknesses in the structure are exposed, during a trial that shakes us, aren't our weaknesses exposed?

After a shaking trial, perhaps our doubts, impatience, fears, pride, or bitterness are exposed. Once they are exposed, we have the opportunity to remove them and allow God to replace them with a stronger faith, more patience, courage, humility, or forgiveness. There may not be joy in the trial, but we can have joy and peace in the anticipated victory over the situation, *"These things I have spoken to you, that in Me you may have peace. In the world, you will have tribulation; but be of good cheer, I have overcome the world,"* John 16:33. We know that through God we can not only withstand the trial, but when we allow God to work we can be made stronger to face the next trial that comes.

REFLECTION

- What trials have you been through? Have any weaknesses been exposed in you as a result of a trial(s)?

- Did you allow God to strengthen those exposed areas?

- According to James 1:2-3 and John 16:33, how are we to act in a trial?

- What perspective can you have with the next trial?

FAITH FOCUS

Walk in faith by joyfully looking
for a victorious outcome over our trials

*"My brethren, count it all joy
when you fall into various trials,
knowing that the testing of your faith
produces patience,"*

James 1:2-3

PRAYER

Heavenly Father, write this Scripture on my heart as I read it out loud and write it in my Faith Notebook.

Heavenly Father, help me to see evidence of this Scripture today.

Record what you see, hear, or experience today that shows evidence of this Scripture.

ENRICHMENT STEP 3
Day 22-31

1. Have you ever had muddy thoughts like in Day 23? I think all humans have had such thoughts. It is not always easy to clean away the mud, but todays exercise may help you remember some steps to cleaning up and keeping the mud away.

You will need;
- A pitcher full of clean water to represent God and His Word.
- Two glasses to represent our minds
- Dirt to represent our negative thoughts
- Pen and paper
- Bible

Focusing on a specific problem, write down at least three negative thoughts you have regarding that problem.

Using the pitcher full of clean water, pour God and His Word into one of the glasses representing your mind. As you say each negative thought, put a hefty spoonful of dirt into the glass. See how cloudy the water has become? You can see how those negative thoughts muddy your thinking.

Write down three Scriptures that identify what God's Word says about your problem.

Again, using the pitcher full of clean water, pour God and His Word into the second glass of water half full. Now, change your focus from the negative, muddy thoughts to God's loving Word and His ability to resolve the problem. Speak each Scripture you wrote as a faith filled thought as you pour more of God's clean water from the pitcher into the glass.

God in His great love for us desires to fill us with His loving Word. When we focus on the muddy thoughts your mind becomes like the muddy glass. Those negative, muddy thoughts can cloud our

137

thinking and fill us with impurities which could make us stressed and sick. However, imagine your mind like the clean glass of God's loving presence and Word. Filling our mind with faith filled thoughts of God's loving Word will give us a clear, joyful thoughts which will nourish our bodies and mind.

2. Identify one area of your life where you would like to strengthen your faith. Write a Scripture verse on a piece of paper that assists you in strengthening your faith in that area of your life. Place that Scripture in a location where you would see it whenever you are confronted with the situation your wish to strengthen.

Here are some examples;

- **Provision** – To strengthen your faith for provision, place the paper with Philippians 4:19 in your wallet by your cash or debit card.

- **Health** – To strengthen your faith for healing, tape the paper with Psalm 103:3 near your medications.

- **Computer or TV** – To strengthen your faith in order to avoid the computer or TV, place the paper with 1 John 4:4 and Philippians 4:13 on your device.

Our loving God wants to fill us with His faith allowing Him to be victorious in all areas of our lives.

In Conclusion Remember ....

Take heart, because whatever you are facing, it is not new to God. He goes before us, and He stands with us through it all. Because God loves us so much, He sent His son, Jesus, who already paid for all of our diseases, pain, and sins when He was crucified on Calvary, 1 John 4:10, Isaiah 53. Now, through Jesus, we are victorious because Jesus rose from the dead, Ephesians 1:19-21.

So, in victorious faith, press forward speaking and acting in faith with single-mindedness. Knowing that God, in His extraordinary love for us will come through in His perfect timing in a way that is His will, for our good and for His glory.

If you are still struggling, ask God to help your unbelief as the father did in Mark 9:24. Continue to build your faith by trusting God with the small stuff. Ask yourself, what little thing can I believe God for today? Asking God to help you with the small stuff will encourage you and build your trust as you see how He answers your prayers. Then take to heart all the blessings and answered prayers no matter how small they are because each small victory we experience will increase our faith.

Remember, God loves you, He is trustworthy, exceedingly able, and through Him nothing is impossible!

"But Jesus looked at them and said, "With men it is impossible, but not with God; for with God all things are possible," Mark 10:27.

If you are unsure whether you know Jesus Christ as your Savior and Lord, I encourage you to pray this prayer:

Dear God,
I recognize that I am a sinner. I am sorry for my sins. Thank you for loving me enough to send Your son, Jesus, to die for the payment for my sins.
As the Bible says, I confess with my mouth the Lord Jesus and believe in my heart that God raised Jesus from the dead. Thank you for saving me.
Help me to follow You in faith from now on.
In Jesus name. Amen

Romans 3:23, Romans 5:8, Romans 10:19

MESSAGE FROM THE AUTHOR

Like many of you, I have had "challenges" in my life. Some challenges defeated me, and some strengthened me. But along the journey with the good and bad, there was an opportunity for my faith to grow.

Perhaps you have experienced some of the same challenges. So, what have I been through to affect my faith? Here are some of the highlights; inability to conceive, miscarriage, difficult pregnancy, a seriously ill child, marriage issues, divorce. Then there were low finances, dating again, remarriage, blended families, extended illness, children, broken trust, congregation split, elderly parent, and the list goes on and on.

We live in an imperfect world, so there will always be challenges. How we react to those challenges and who we depend on will determine the amount of peace we have as we walk through them. I pray as you take this journey; you will grow your faith and increase your peace.

Diane Bewer Lese

Make sure to check out Diane's website and blog: https://dianelese.com

Thanks to all those who have encouraged me in my journey of faith.

- Grove Avenue Baptist Church congregation
- Be In Health ministry
- Rabbi Jamie Cowen
- Or HaOlam Congregation
- Brian Wills
- Bishop Greg Brewer
- Jo Wade
- Barbara Duchin
- And so many others along the way

Special thanks to those who not only encouraged me but contributed to this book:

- My husband, Alan Lese
- My daughter, Jacquelyn "Jackie" Pitts
- My friend, Anne Clark
- My publisher and editor, Bill and Nancy James
- And my cover designer Megan Dillon

www.ingramcontent.com/pod-product-compliance
Lightning Source LLC
Chambersburg PA
CBHW030307130626
46549CB00002B/734